WINDING
TRAIL
PRESS

Transcending

Trauma

RUTH MORRIS
with
Ruth Bradley-St-Cyr

WINDING
TRAIL
PRESS

WINDING TRAIL PRESS
1304 St-Jacques Rd.
Embrun, Ontario KOA 1WO Canada
ruthbear@ca.inter.net

The names Bail-Out Program, Half-Way Society, George, Bob,
Lila, and Francine are fictitious.

Library and Archives Canada Cataloguing in Publication

Morris, Ruth, 1933–
   Transcending trauma / Ruth Morris with Ruth Bradley-St-Cyr.

Includes bibliographical references.
ISBN 0-9733632-4-X

1. Grief. 2. Death—Psychological aspects. 3. Cancer—Psychological aspects.
4. Life change events—Religious aspects. I. Bradley-St-Cyr, Ruth, 1962– II. Title.

BJ1487.M67 2005   155.9'3   C2005-900129-1

The Winding Trail Press logo is based on the logo of the Ryerson
Press, designed by Thoreau MacDonald

Publisher: Ruth Bradley-St-Cyr
Art Director: Laura Brady
Copy editing: David Bernardi
Printer: AGMV Marquis

1 2 3 4 5 6 7 8 9 10 11 AGMV 12 11 10 09 08 07 06 05

CONTENTS

We are afflicted in every way, but not crushed;
Perplexed but not driven to despair;
Persecuted, but not forsaken;
Struck down, but not destroyed.

— 2 CORINTHIANS 4: 8-9

To Ray Morris for his unfailing love, support, generosity and humor, and for making life one long blessing.

—Ruth Morris

To my husband, Baudouin St-Cyr, who has shared my journey through all the traumas and victories. And to my grandmother, Edna Bradley, who has transcended many traumas over her hundred and two years (so far).

—Ruth Bradley-St-Cyr

Foreword

IN EARLY 2001, MY AUNT, Ruth Rittenhouse Morris, and her husband, Ray, retired from their jobs and moved to Salmon Arm, British Columbia, from Toronto, where they had lived for 40 years. She was battling kidney cancer. One June morning, she announced over the phone how she thought it was time to check into the local hospital. Determined to keep strong, she admitted that eating was a bigger problem than the cancer itself. We spoke lightly of this step, but we both knew it was backwards progress. Her good-bye was shaky.

Three hours later, she called back breathlessly, "You'll never guess what happened!" She explained how just as she and Ray got into their car to go to the hospital a man arrived with a telegram. It wasn't the Publisher's Clearinghouse Prize team, but it was important news from Canada's Governor General. In recognition for her pioneering work to transform the criminal justice system, Ruth had been awarded the Order of Canada, the country's highest honor for public service. All thoughts of the hospital vanished. She and Ray went back in the house to phone family and friends with the news.

On July 30, the Lieutenant Governor of British Columbia drove up to their home with attendants and caterers and threw a party for Ruth's investiture. (The formal installation in Ottawa was still some months away, but Ruth's friends worried that her illness might prevent her from attending.) Ruth wore a long flowing dress, the color of burnt clay. Framed by a view of the evergreen-studded mountains that circle the shores of Salmon Arm's vast blue Shuswap Lake, she accepted the medal in a room overflowing with family and friends. She talked about her vision for us all to create the beloved community.

More than anyone I've known, Ruth, supported by her husband Ray, lived to do good. She worked ceaselessly to create social justice in our world. She was a champion of the power of forgiveness. To see her struggle with cancer just at the time when she and Ray dreamed of starting their new life together in Salmon Arm seemed liked a bad cosmic joke. How could this champion of justice be treated so unjustly?

But cancer didn't stop Ruth. As always, she shared her journey, the mountains *and* the valleys, with those fortunate to walk with her. Characteristically, she found a new mission in this struggle. She challenged the inhumanity of conventional medicine and doctors trained in mind and body, but not soul medicine. She also supported people with cancer who have fewer resources in their battle. In hindsight, I can now see that she championed another more elusive cause.

Ruth lived each day with the awareness of not knowing when her time would be up. Like the characters in Thornton Wilder's play, *Our Town*, she knew how blind our sight-filled eyes can be. When the character Emily dies giving birth to her child, she gets the chance to relive one day of her life on Earth. She chooses her twelfth birthday. As she watches her mother cook breakfast and talk to her twelve-year-old self, the ghost of Emily cries out, "Oh, Mama, just look at me one minute as though you really saw me. Just for a moment now we're all together, Mama. Just for a moment we're happy. Let's look at one another." Turning to the audience she says, "It goes too fast." She begins to cry, "Take me back to my grave. But first: Wait! One more look…"

I used to wonder why we all couldn't live with Emily's awareness. Now I think I understand how unsettling this is. Living each day knowing how precious life is confronts us with its impermanence. We begin to see that all we love can be lost in an instant. It's safer to go back to our possessions and our waking unconsciousness. Ruth's struggle with cancer is her gift to us: *the courage to live each day fully knowing it could be our last.*

Ruth challenges us to see how our lives are improved unexpectedly, even miraculously, precisely because of the unseen gifts hidden in the traumas we face. But she never pretended that healing and forgiveness were easy work. She knew what warriors of the spirit need: listening ears tuned to the highest empathetic frequencies; an ability to laugh at life's absurdities; an unshakable belief in God's grace and an open, nonjudgmental heart that can pierce through fierce defenses and embrace our pure spirits.

Ruth died on September 16, five days after September 11, 2001. Hundreds of people came to a Quaker memorial service in Toronto a few weeks after her death; many got up to speak. One woman rose saying that Ruth described herself as someone destined to "fail gloriously." She knew that my aunt was in the business of growing her soul and not her bank account. After she sat down, a man stood and cleared his throat before speaking. "I never met Ruth Morris," he said, "but I am here because I just returned from the International Conference on Penal Abolition (ICOPA), a group she started 18 years ago. This year," he continued, "700 people met to find ways to bring about transformative justice. Everyone was talking about Ruth Morris." He said, "She did not fail."

Others spoke about carrying on her work. In fact, tributes to my aunt poured in from around the world. I've collected these in a book that shows the difference one life can make. A favorite quote came from my cousin Beverly describing how she saw Ruth's influence in the world: "On the day you were born, you cried and the world rejoiced. Live your life in such a way that on the day you die, the world will cry and you will rejoice."

I invite you to read some of these glorious tributes (pages xi to xiii). They are testaments that show how Ruth helped to remind us of the choice we make each day: to risk or not to risk loving. Ruth's life was a testament choosing to risk loving no matter what. By her example, she showed that when we confront and even befriend our fears, we find the rare gifts of community, simplicity, and the clarity that love *is* all there is. These tributes show how deeply Ruth touched those lucky enough to be in her orbit. At the same time, these tributes need a warning label. I challenge anyone to read them and not ask, "How am I using my time?"

Five days after the terrorist attacks in New York City, where I live, my daughter and I escaped to the country to stay with friends. That afternoon, I sat by a lake enjoying the quiet and watching the sun make stars on the blue-green water. Suddenly two brilliant monarch butterflies came to dance before me. I thought, "Is Ruth telling me it is her time?" She died later that day. My minister smiled when he heard this story. "Amazing," he said, "her soul was so big it needed two butterflies to carry it home."

LAURA RITTENHOUSE
Author of Do Business with
People You Can Trust:
Balancing Profits and Principles

A Bouquet of Tributes

Ruth was one of the few people I have encountered who – instead of running away from or distancing or shooshing people who are in crisis or whose worlds have been turned upside down by personal loss or public humiliation or social rejection – could meet you during these moments with no iota of condescension.

She could acknowledge the pain while gently making the case for hope in the most convincing way possible. I listened to Ruth – even if not fully convinced – because I felt that her hope was itself born of a courageous struggle against despair and cruelty and the mean-spiritedness she saw around her. Somehow she managed to forgive and understand without denying its existence – as so many others seem to do.

Even though I did not know Ruth well at the time of my wife's untimely death, she was one of the very few people who did not make me feel ashamed or embarrassed by the dark and despairing feelings I was experiencing at the time. In this way, I was touched by her as I now understand she touched many others.

—RICHARD WEISMAN, criminologist,
ICOPA participant, colleague of Ray Morris

I have been blessed to know Ruth, and to learn from her. Her voice is inside me, her words run through my blood. Through Rittenhouse, I have a path that she has guided me onto.

In my own tradition, it is the Days of Awe, the period spanning Rosh Hashanah and Yom Kippur. I have always noticed that those who have lived their lives most intensely die at this time of year – the ripest time, the fullest time of the year. These days give me a special opportunity to reflect on Ruth's life, and bless the ways in which she contributed to *tikkum olam* – a repairing of the world.

—MARILYN EISENSTAT, ICOPA organizer,
Rittenhouse Board member, dear friend

Ruth has described her life goal as follows – "to use my talents to bring healing and wholeness to those who fall into the cracks of society, and to grow in transforming negative events into positive energy toward a society which includes all of its members." In pursuit of her objective, Ruth has demonstrated remarkable qualities of leadership, especially vision. Undoubtedly, this significant talent is founded in her high principles and her deep spirituality.

However significant has been this exercise of vision – and it as been very significant – she does more than theorize and teach. She consistently rolls up her sleeves, applies those principles and shows others how the destructiveness of poverty, homelessness, incarceration, and racism may be addressed.

Ruth's contributions, more often than not, have been unique. Had she not taken the initiative on many of her projects, the social good produced may not have materialized at all. Unfortunately, there are not enough Ruth Morrises.

—GARFIELD MAHOOD, excerpted from his letter
to nominate Ruth for The Order of Canada

Ruth has again used the wind blowing in this world, to rise above with faith that's secure. Ruth once used this idea on the use of power described by E. Stanley Jones: "When a storm strikes an eagle, it does not fight the storm with the power of its wings; rather it spreads its wings, and uses the very fury of the storm to rise above it." The storm has passed in her life now, and she has risen beyond this world and now gone into God's presence.

—DON and SHARON RENDLE, Canadian pastors
and crusaders in Latin American prisons

My Aunt Ruth was a fiery ball of energy – her sheer joy for life, her all-encompassing love, and her laughter and wonderful sense of humor that she could find in almost any situation. She was like Glinda, the Good Witch of Oz, using her magic wand to transform people, situations, hate or fear to love. She was a fearless warrior making the world a better place, one person at a time.

—EILEEN RITTENHOUSE BOWEN, daughter of
Ruth's brother, Bob, Buffalo, New York

My life has been enriched through knowing Ruth. She saw good and potential in everyone. She enabled me to do things I never imagined I could or would. She encouraged and inspired me. She was unselfish and inclusive, compassionate and willing to take risks! She was humble and gave credit where due.

—BEATRICE O'BYRNE, former employee

We will miss your prophetic voice, your words of comfort, your challenges to the principalities and powers, and your "sense of daring" – that willingness to walk toward your opponents rather than backing away, inspiring others to face, with courage, the real challenges of dealing with injustices in our day to day living.

Thank you for whom you have been and what you have meant. Thank you for the courage and the hope that you expressed in the midst of all the questions and wonderments about the tumor and about what the future would hold. Thank you for the ways in which you brought new meaning and value to life even as you looked death in the face.

I am richer in many ways because our lives have touched, and I will be ever grateful for that privilege.

—DALTON JANTZI, Mennonite community worker,
member of long-time spiritual support group

They that love beyond the world
Cannot be separated by it.
Death cannot kill what never dies,
Nor can spirits ever be divided
That love and live in the same divine principle.

If absence be not death,
Neither is theirs...
For they must needs be present
That love and live in that which is omnipresent.

—William Penn

FINISHING A BOOK FOR SOMEONE ELSE is a rather delicate business. It's not my book, after all, it's Ruth Morris' book. After Ruth died I could feel her, standing behind my right shoulder as I worked on the book. Her presence was so strong that I felt I needed to explain, out loud, my reasons for moving something or deleting a particular word.

———

Just two weeks before Ruth died I was preaching at the little church near our cottage about *Transcending Trauma*. It was only the fourth church service I have ever led. Obviously, I am not an experienced preacher. My usual

———

method would be to start writing the sermon weeks in advance, revising it over and over. This time, I found it almost impossible to get the sermon prepared, as there were so many other demands on my time. In the end, in frustration and worried about doing a bad job, I vowed to get up very early on the Sunday morning to write it.

That night I dreamt about Ruth. There was a church service she needed to be at – perhaps the one I was preaching at – and I was determined to be there to support her. It was quite far from home for both of us. Ruth had arrived the night before the service and had slept in a park close to the church. Only I could see her as she slept. Someone sat on her by accident.

She was covered with a blanket of snow and her face was all puffy and bruised because she had slept right next to a metal post and had been accidentally banging into it as she slept. Her face looked like one of those dolls you make out of old pantyhose. She was much the worse for her night of sleeping rough.

The service was about to begin so it was time to wake her up. I went over to her and cupped her face in my hands and said "Ruth, I'm here." She said, "It's you" and smiled. As I held her face, the skin seemed to smooth back into place and she seemed to recover.

In my dream Ruth chose to sleep, battered and bruised, in a park under a blanket of snow precisely because that is a fate that so many people endure. When I looked into her face I saw all anguish and torture and destitution. She had taken all that upon herself in order to make a difference in the world.

That dream became the core of my sermon. It was like a gift that Ruth had given to me as I slept. That sermon pretty much wrote itself.

———

Two days after my sermon I found myself out of a job. The owner of the publishing house I had worked at for two years fired me for no reason and with no warning. It was a very bitter blow, especially considering that my husband was in the middle of a two-year, unpaid leave and I was the sole breadwinner for our family of five. For a while, I forgot the lessons Ruth had taught me about using tragedy for transformation and became engaged in a legal battle. Our overly litigious society has made such things normal. In the process we have become blinded to the fact that you really can't win a legal battle. Like the estate held in chancery for a hundred years in Dickens' *Bleak House*, it is only the lawyers who win, in the end. The estate itself trickles away to pay legal bills until there isn't a penny left.

As I recovered a bit from the body blow of being fired, I recalled the words of my own sermon, taken from Ruth's book, about risking love again and about forgiveness. I began to heal. In fact, I came to feel grateful for the firing, for it released me from a very unhealthy workplace and offered instead whole new experiences and wonderful new colleagues.

I even had a dream about my former boss. In my dream he apologized for his treatment of me by saying that he had to empty out my office because he needed to move his grandparents in there. This probably makes as much sense as the real explanation, since the grandparents are long since dead. In any case, the bitterness lifted from me and I moved on.

Since then my husband got a new job, we've moved to a new town, my brother got married, one friend had a car accident, another friend had a baby, my grandmother turned one hundred and two, my mother-in-law died, I've preached several times more . . . in short, the usual ups and downs of life have taken over again.

———

At the time I started editing Ruth's book I had to deal with the news about Ruth's own cancer but I also had another friend facing a brain tumor. I didn't know what I could do for my friend. It seemed pretty hopeless. This was a recurrence of a tumor that had been removed several years before. It seemed to be inoperable and fatal, although she is still with us as I write this.

I avoided calling her for a long time – about a year actually – because it all seemed so hopeless. I kept having fears, however, that my friend would die and that no one would tell me about it. And then I read Ruth's words in this book: "Do something, not nothing" and "You do the reaching." I put aside my embarrassment at not calling for so long and just did it. As it turns out, over the year many more problems had come to her family. Her inevitable death was ripping her family apart. Her sons were both failing school and suicidal and her husband had been charged with child abuse for kicking one of them. There was something I could do for her, however. "I just want to get out of this house for a while," she told me. We went to lunch.

But I have to keep reminding myself that one lunch, like one sympathy card, is not enough. I have to reach out again and again and that, even if I do this, I can't fix my friend's problems. But I can listen to them and help her a little in that small way.

———

One could say that Ruth Morris approached illness and death stoically and bravely, but the truth is that she approached it with the same joy and passion that she put into everything else she did in her life.

In that dream I had about her the night before my sermon, Ruth was a famous potter. She was not very careful with her pots, leaving them lying all over the place. I found a couple of them sitting, unwrapped, in the back of my car. These gifts were everywhere, awaiting only the awareness of the finder that they were precious. In reaching out to share her own experiences of trauma, Ruth has become a great teacher. She has left us all the lessons in this book, like the exquisite pots in my dreams, strewn everywhere for us to find and pick up and carry away with us.

RUTH BRADLEY-ST-CYR
Embrun, Ontario
March 2005

CHAPTER 1

The Challenge: Why We Aren't Prepared

For sorrow and suffering are not things to run away from, but to live through and understand... For I see more and more that all the great souls must go through this shadow and find the sunlight beyond. But my dear little Lois, you don't understand this yet, and don't try to. The time will come when you can . . .

—THOMAS KELLY, letter to his 10-year-old daughter

THE TIME HAS COME. We're not children anymore. We have to deal with trauma now. You wouldn't have picked up this book if you didn't. Why do we feel so bad when bad things happen? Because we are all locked into two destructive myths:

Myth One: Tragedy won't come to me unless I am careless or bad.

Myth Two: A one-shot Hallmark card is the all-sufficient answer to any tragedy — for brave people get over tragedy immediately.

This realization came to me the day Jan walked into my office. She was a new acquaintance, not even a friend. But I knew her husband had gone into hospital for some tests earlier that week, and she was ashy white. I invited her in, helped her find a comfortable seat, offered her something to drink, and then turned my whole focus of attention on her. "What's happened, Jan?" I asked. "How is Ted?"

She didn't plunge straight to a final answer. "They did the tests on Tuesday," she began. "It took two days to get the results."

"It must have been ghastly for both of you, waiting," I observed, and again waited for her to continue in her own time, in her own way.

She paused, more because she was stunned and withdrawn than choking back emotion. But after a bit she went on, "It's a tumor. And it's grown. And there is nothing they can do."

For a moment I was too surprised to think of her. I was overwhelmed by my own shock. How could this be? Jan and Ted were not bad people out of step with the Lord. They were a young couple in their late twenties, just finishing their education, just beginning personal and professional ventures to heal the world's ills. This couldn't be happening to them!

I expressed my shock and grief and sympathy with my face and only a few words. It felt as flat as a sympathy card. Then I got hold of myself. I remembered Jan had the greater need here and that my needs should be subordinate to hers. I also knew that in meeting her needs, I would be contributing to my own forward movement in dealing with this terrible shock. I put aside my other plans on that busy day, and sat quietly, patiently, trying to absorb her mood, her needs. I wanted to respond to where she was at, not to my perception of where she should or might be. I focussed all my attention on really *listening* to her. If I knew a similar experience that seemed to me to have a perfect answer, but it didn't seem to be helpful to her, I exercised the enormous discipline of dropping it, and returned to listening for cues to her needs, her story, her feelings. It was hard work, but rewarding, and it was healing for us both.

Jan's story is a terrible challenge for her, for Ted, and for everyone whose lives theirs touch. But it is just one of many tragedies each of us will face in the course of our lives. In the Middle Ages, in Far Eastern cultures, in Biblical times, in fact in most times and places — including our own time in the developing world — tragic suffering was so widespread that people had better, more systematic and appropriate ways of dealing with it. When families routinely lost half or more of their children to infant mortality or childhood diseases, there was no illusion that death was an issue one could avoid.

We may try to fool ourselves into thinking that grief hits "us" harder than it hit "them" because it is less expected. One impossible to follow piece of advice from bygone times was that parents should not grow too attached to their children until they reached the age of fourteen, lest they lose them. English poet Ben Jonson (1573–1637) lost his first-born son and his first-born daughter in childhood and wrote heart-wrenching poems to both of them. His son Benjamin — meaning "son of my right hand" (Genesis 35:18) — died of the plague on his seventh birthday in 1603:

On My First Son

Farewell, thou child of my right hand, and joy;
    My sin was too much hope of thee, loved boy.
Seven years thou wert lent to me, and I thee pay,
    Exacted by thy fate, on the just day.
Oh, could I lose all father now! For why
    Will man lament the state he should envy?
To have so soon 'scaped world's and flesh's rage,
    And if no other misery, yet age!
Rest in soft peace, and asked, say, Here doth lie
    Ben Jonson his best piece of poetry.
For whose sake henceforth all his vows be such
    As what he loves may never like to much.

If grief was not less painful, however, it was usually borne more stoically out of sheer necessity than we bear ours today. One key to this was that there was more of a shared base of religious faith — there were relevant answers most people agreed on, and worked together to affirm in times of tragedy, as Jonson's poem to his daughter, who died in infancy around 1598, shows:

On My First Daughter

Here lies, to each her parents' ruth,
Mary, the daughter of their youth;
Yet, all heaven's gifts being heaven's due,

It makes the father less to rue.
At six months' end she parted hence
With safety of her innocence;
Whose soul heaven's Queen (whose name she bears)
In comfort of her mother's tears,
Hath placed amongst her virgin-train:
Where, while the severed doth remain,
This grave partakes the fleshly birth,
Which cover lightly, gentle earth.

It is only in modern, science-saved Western 20th century culture that we have both gained and lost so much. We have gained wonderful ways of saving lives and of using our skills to give us technological wonders: cars, radios, televisions, dishwashers, computers, airplanes, space travel, telephones, vacuum cleaners, the Internet... The list goes on and on. But with our advances, we have lost something precious: a common religious faith to help us deal with tragedy, and a community that knows how to care for its most afflicted members. We have added electric wheelchairs, and have lost the gift of caring, patient, accepting, empathetic listening. We have developed technology that can keep our bodies alive long after our minds have lost touch with this world and have lost the extended family circle that gathers around a dying loved one. We have created a faith in our own man-made science and lost the shared faith that celebrates the passing from this world to the next — to the realm of the spirit.

Lacking a common faith to respond to tragedies as unanswerable as Jan's, we wall ourselves off from reality. Let's look at those two myths again:

Myth One: Tragedy won't come to me unless I am careless or bad.

Myth Two: A one-shot Hallmark card is the all-sufficient answer to any tragedy — for brave people get over tragedy immediately.

These two myths arise partly out of our lost faith, but partly out of our false gods of science and technology. If modern methods can conquer all for us, then trauma should not happen; or, as the Russian writer Maxim Gorky asserted, "In a planned and classless society, a streetcar would not run over a beautiful girl." The prolonged reality of grieving reminds us uncomfortably that our false gods have failed us. Before we can look at healthier responses, we need to look at our two widely accepted but destructive social myths in more depth.

Myth One: It Can't Happen to Me

> Is there anyone who has everything as he wishes? No — neither you, nor I, nor any man on earth. There is no one in the world, be he Pope or king, who does not suffer trial or anguish. Who is the better off then? Surely it is the man who will suffer something *for God* . . .
>
> — GERHARD GROOTE, *The Imitation of Christ*

We are grounded in the faith that the ideal Western family has 2.2 children, an idyllic marriage, a suburban home with an affordable mortgage, full employment, and no serious conflicts. The present fifty percent divorce rate might seem to challenge this, but we manage to maintain the idyllic family myth and the awareness that family life is in trouble in separate compartments most of the time. Furthermore, we continue a similar faith in the myth of our invulnerability.

This mythical "average family" never experiences serious illness, accidents, bereavement, alcoholism, abuse, mental illness, depression, miscarriage, unemployment, family break-up, delinquent children, conflict with the law, failure, or any other shock. If we allow ourselves to think about death at all, we expect to die peacefully in our beds at the age of at least 88. That's the way we are socialized to think it is supposed to be. Set down in black and white, it is not just an appallingly dull and colorless existence, it is positively silly. Are all friends and relations required to die simultaneously, to spare us the experience of bereavement?

But it is worse than silly. This myth is terribly destructive, for it leads us to rage and blame endlessly when trauma does inevitably strike. If it strikes us, we blame God (even if we never before acknowledged God's existence,

S/He's in for it now!). We also blame anyone within firing distance. And we blame ourselves. If trauma strikes others, God gets it again, but most of the rest of the blame goes to the victim: they *must* have done something wrong, or it couldn't have happened to them.

This response is aggravated when the trauma is job loss, unemployment, or an accident in which the victim could, even if only theoretically, have done something differently. I have run workshops for the unemployed in which we had a wonderful time role playing the responses of friends to their situations. "But the want ads have columns of jobs, Sue. Why can't you get busy and get one of them?" Such responses ignore the fact that all the jobs may be in sales or clerical areas, and that Sue has neither ability nor qualifications in either. It also ignores realities such as the fact that there are 35,000 people in any large city actively seeking the 100 jobs in those "long columns of ads." But it is so much easier to blame Sue, and others in her shoes, than to face the scary reality that unemployment is a big threat in our society, and that it can happen to any of us. It has often been said that much of the middle class is only a couple of paychecks from being on the street.

With an accident, people may be more likely to talk behind the back of the person. "Well, I wouldn't say it to Mike," a friend remarks, "But I have told him many times he should have bought a heavier car. Those light ones are deathtraps, and if he had been driving a solid car when the truck hit him, he wouldn't be in hospital today!" Unfeeling as these comments sound (and are), they are sadly typical of the voiced or unvoiced reactions of many people in our society. We run away from the truth that trauma can happen to anybody by finding any excuse at all to blame the victim. What is almost worse, we blame ourselves for the same reasons. A part of us keeps saying, "I must have done *something wrong*, or my child would not have been born with this handicap."

However, modern Western society doesn't have any monopoly on this distorted response. Job's friends in the Bible kept telling Job that he must have done something wrong. Blaming the victim is an old and cherished device for avoiding the truth that bad things *do* happen to good people. It's just that we've perfected it to a systematic and destructive ritual. We, too, often blame our friends for their troubles. If they are to blame for them, then we don't have to face the fact that such troubles could happen to us! The reality of the troubles of these good people threatens our whole faith in the belief that if we are good and careful and organized and scientific, we won't experience tragedy ourselves.

Mind you, some raging against the trauma is a healthy part of the grieving process. The "*Why Mes*" and the "*If Onlys*" are part of searching for any preventive learning we need to gain, and part of coming to grips with the terrible new reality in our lives. It's just that we moderns have put all our energy for far too long into beating our souls against the rock of the inevitable, seeking to *blame* instead of to *accept*. Science can change many things, but it cannot bring a dead child back to life, heal a broken marriage, or give the victim of a cruel firing back their faith in a just and reliable employment world. Accepting the inevitability and the universality of trauma helps us cope with it in healthier ways, when it affects us or those we love. And affect us it will — down to the last human being.

The *bad* news is that every one of us, every person reading this book and every person who avoids reading anything about trauma or grief, will suffer not just one but many traumas in their lives. Grief, illness, accident, family trouble, these and other traumas visit all of us. Yet, we foolishly raise our children in an effort to shield them from all pain, instead of helping them learn how to cope with pain. In reality, children are often better able than we are to grasp spiritual truths, if they are exposed to them. A minister at my father's memorial service told us about how a friend of his five-year-old daughter had been killed, and how he was worried about how to tell his daughter. He finally gave her the news the best he could, and watched her anxiously.

"Is she with Jesus?" the child asked innocently.

"Yes, she is," the father replied.

"Well then, she's all right!" his daughter replied serenely, and went on about her life, undaunted. Children can deal with the toughest challenges of life if we share with them, help them to grow, and support them. Children like that little girl can help us cope in a more appropriate way, as well. It is right that we protect our children and not let them feel abandoned in times of trauma; but it is wrong that we try to pretend it does not exist, or that good deeds are always rewarded in this world.

7

By overprotecting them, we convey our excessive fear of their fragility.

The most precious of all the precious gifts my mother shared with me was her pain in dealing with my Dad's emotional limitations. She never burdened me with it beyond what I could deal with, but she trusted me as a member of the family whom she could work together with in building solutions. That trust gave me the roots of the strength that has enabled me to deal with all my adult traumas creatively, with God's help.

My own daughter, Corinne, reinforced this lesson for me when I was reading *The Forsyte Saga* to her and I mistakenly imagined that I needed to explain a remark of one of the characters to my wise twelve-year-old daughter. A main character, who was a socialist, was going to get married, and some of his friends were joshing him that that would cure him of his socialism. I turned to Corinne and explained, "That's because when people become parents, they start wanting to pass things on to their children."

She looked at me in surprise and asked with an innocent wisdom, which I have never forgotten, "But Mom, why don't parents realize that the most important things they have to pass on to their children are their *values?*" Why not indeed! We should never underestimate the wisdom of children, and their potential to teach us as well as vice versa.

The *good* news is that God offers the same love and support, the same divine grace in this age as God has offered to the great saints, martyrs, and prophets who have faced deep suffering through the ages. The good news is that you can learn from trauma and grow through it. This book contains hints from people who have gotten into closer touch with that wonderful, sustaining, comforting grace, and have become deeper, more alive, more caring human beings through trauma.

There is even more good news: lonely as the journey of grief is, we *can* help one another on it. While we need to get in touch with the spirit of God within each of us, and not try to get all our spiritual support second hand by draining our friends, the love of friends is an incredible help when it is sensitively shared. Many in deep trauma have cried out, "I could not have made it this far without the love and support of so many friends who cared. The one thing that gave life continued meaning was the reaching out of the many loved ones who stretched a hand to me through the blackness of my despair." All of us would like to be that kind of friend. One purpose of this book is to help you be such a friend to your loved ones in their times of deepest need.

Myth Two: You'll Get Over It Soon

> For the accomplishment of love is suffering, voluntarily taken on oneself, and he who has not loved has not lived, and he who has not lived has not suffered . . .
> — THOMAS KELLY, *Testament of Devotion*

Sending a card or giving a call to someone in trauma is wonderful — but it is just a beginning! The closer you are to the center of the trauma, the longer it takes to complete the cycle:

Shock — Grief — Acceptance — Healing and Reintegration

Those on the outer fringes of the catastrophe go through the whole cycle in a few days. They make their one call to those at the storm center, and are surprised when that person is not A-OK in a week or a month. But when you are at the center of a major grief or trauma, the phases take years. The different time clocks add conflicts and misunderstandings to the already high stress of those most affected, as Table 1 shows.

TABLE 1: Times Different Sufferers Move Through the Cycles			
Relation to the Trauma	*Stages of Trauma*		
Victims	Shock	Grief-Acceptance	Healing-Reintegration
Friends	S/G-A	H-R	
Witnesses	S/G-A/H-R		
Time Taken in Each Stage	1-3 mos.	3 mos. to 2 years	2 to 4 years

What this little table illustrates is that people are out of synch with each other: bystanders are over it before friends even get out of shock and into grief. As for the primary victim, everyone else is ready to get on with his or her life by the time the victim has come out of the protective numbness of shock into the full anguish of grief. The cry from all around the victim is "What's wrong with you? Don't be such a whiner! You should be getting over this by now. Quit moping and get on with your life!" So, the victim has added to his/her burden the choice of carrying all that pain silently within, or of being labeled a coward, a failure, and a misfit. But there is nothing wrong with needing support over a period of years. In fact, much literature on grief estimates that the average time for moving through the major stages of shock and grief in a significant trauma is two to four years.

Yet, even this is a dangerous figure, for every grief for every person has its own time, and no one should feel guilty about working through the process in their own way. Moreover, in a sense, one is never done with a major trauma. Just as a lost limb affects the rest of one's life, so does a lost child. Rape has also been shown to have a lifelong impact. So do unemployment, alcoholism, and divorce.

Even for those far along the recovery road, a new hit on the old wound, such as the anniversary of a death, rape, accident, or firing, is a challenge each year. Some healthy families find ceremonies helpful to share on the anniversary of a death. A Catholic friend of mine writes out a worship service that she and her children share on the anniversary of her husband's death. One very mature mother of a teenaged suicide victim observed, "I've made enormous progress now. After five years, I can sometimes go fifteen minutes without thinking about it." So much for the destructive myth of the instant fix.

In fact there are many walking wounded in the world — some who never leave the wilderness of grief and venture, via acceptance, into the terrain of healing and reintegration. For example, after Tom's father died on Tom's 32nd birthday he never celebrated his birthday again. Tom himself died — much too young — at the age of 59. He had never really accepted the death and moved on and thus shortened his own life in the process. One study of centenarians showed that being able to roll with the punches of life was essential to their longevity. The average 100-year-old will have lost a spouse, parents, siblings, cousins, most, if not all, of their friends, and even some of their children and grandchildren.

What is the solution? The solution is to accept that trauma is a long lesson in the school of life. The cost is patient, loving support throughout the process that encourages the person to talk it out and share it. The gains are great. Eventually, with support from others, the trauma becomes a lesson in spiritual growth, instead of a festering wound.

We must remember that those in the center need people reaching to them. They need respect, and having others reach to them empowers them as equals. Recently I explained to a friend that I would appreciate it if *she* would call *me* during a hard time in my life. She said in surprise, "But you can call me anytime." I had to explain to her that most traumas are disempowering and make you feel isolated. Reaching for help is hard and makes you feel dependent. Having help reach out to you makes you feel valued, needed, cared for, and respected. But most help, if offered at all, is of the "call-me-if-you-need-me" variety.

At the same time, it is terribly important to recognize and accept individual differences, as I learned when I gave support to a friend dying of cancer. Sarah was young (under forty) and in terrible physical pain. She was worried about her sister, Caroline, who was fairly isolated in the world and under other stresses. Both Sarah and Caroline were going through deep and terrible traumas. My instinct was to pour on support, to talk openly about the deep subjects, to call daily, to visit, and to invite others who know them to join in this circle of support. In fact, each of them is different, and needed support in different ways. Sarah would talk about death and about her sister's needs with me, but was horrified at involving anyone beyond our small circle in her situation. She was, as both Sarah and Caroline kept telling me, "a very private person." Caroline, on the other hand, while respecting Sarah's need for privacy and helping me to understand it better, was devastated that it put a wall, at times, between them in the last weeks they could share.

My responsibility was to listen actively to the needs of each of these sisters, to respect the shock they were dealing with, and to support them in coping with it in their own ways. Because my way is to be more open, I had to stretch my understanding to respond to Sarah's way. Yet these differences don't change the fundamental reality: Sarah and Caroline both needed reliable support and sensitive listening — which, for Caroline, would stretch far beyond the weeks of her sister's dying. They were not to blame for

Sarah's illness, nor the stress it put them under, nor the unreasonable demands the disease made on them and all close to them. Sarah's illness was one of those hard challenges of life, and her friends had the choice of running away from it by avoiding or blaming the victims (both Sarah and Caroline), or growing from it to become more empathetic, deeply spiritual, and valuable people.

In short, the myth of the quick fix leads most of us who do reach out to do it only once, and do it early on. This still leaves those experiencing trauma to feel isolated, for there are long, hard years of grief and reintegration still ahead.

Stages of Trauma

> I am not alone in my tiredness or sickness or fears, but at one with millions of others from many centuries. It is all part of life . . .
>
> —ETTY HILLESUM, An Interrupted Life

The remainder of this book, with the assistance of many wise people, as well as my own personal experiences, is a guide for moving through the four major stages of trauma:

- Shock
- Grief
- Acceptance
- Healing and Reintegration

The even-numbered chapters — two, four, six, and eight — talk first about what the sufferer can do for her/himself, then about what friends can do to support that struggle. Chapter Two addresses shock and its duel with denial. Chapter Four deals with the long journey of grief. Grief is the longest and in many ways the hardest stage. Acceptance signals a turning point in the journey of grief — the point at which one can move onto the path of healing. Chapter Six deals with acceptance. Chapter Eight talks about the final stage, which comprises of healing, forgiveness, and reintegration.

The odd-numbered chapters – three, five, seven, and nine — deal with my own personal traumas, which illustrate what I've learned about trauma and how I've learned it. Chapter Three introduces my first major trauma, job loss, and some of the lessons I learned and applied to subsequent traumas — another job loss and two bouts with cancer. Chapter Five is my own personal parable; a story of my journey through a dark time. This was my second workplace trauma, and it illustrates the things that helped, and the things that didn't. Chapters Seven and Nine are the most recent story: the journey of my wonderful family and friends who accompanied me through my final struggle with cancer.

Finally, Chapter Ten reminds us that trauma too has gifts for us, and that part of accepting trauma lies in seeing and welcoming the rich gifts hidden in its hard lessons. To all of you who read this book, welcome to the greatest challenges life offers — the challenges of trauma, grief, and failure. Through their dark passages, you can tune into a richer, fuller symphony of living than you ever dreamed of before you encountered this painful and unwanted experience.

> Most of us in the West don't understand the art of suffering, and experience fears instead. We cease to be alive, being full of fear, bitterness, hatred, and despair... Does it matter if it is the Inquisition that causes people to suffer in one century, and war and pogroms in another? Suffering has always been with us. Does it really matter in what form it comes?
>
> All that matters is how we bear it, and how we fit it into our lives.
>
> —ETTY HILLESUM, An Interrupted Life

CHAPTER 2

Shock: It's Not Real!

Suffering is difficult to define. Basically it is something (maybe quite minor) which happens against our will, is unpleasant, and blows our carefully regulated lives asunder. We protest, kicking and screaming for the restoration of the status quo ante. If we can persuade ourselves to stop struggling and come to terms with the pain, adapt our natural rhythms to it, accept it as no better and no worse than it is, we may still be foundering in darkness, but the darkness may contain the promise of light.

— MARY CRAIG, *Blessings*

WHEN TRAGEDY FIRST STRIKES us, our overwhelming reactions are horror and a sense of unreality. "This can't be real!" we say to ourselves numbly. Or "It can't be happening to me!" The shock experience itself is terribly real, but the essence of shock is that it enables us to deny the reality of our trauma and to absorb it little by little, day after day. The inability to take it in fully saves us from being buried in the tidal wave of the full long-term impact it will have on us. The denial that Kubler-Ross identifies as the first stage of adjustment to death by the terminally ill exactly corresponds to the denial of a new victim of any major trauma. In both cases, it is necessary in order to let us take the new truth in manageable portions. But it leads to some strange reactions.

When I brought flowers to a friend who had just been through the most brutal firing experience I have ever witnessed, he and his wife kept half smiling with that strange nervous smile that often characterizes those in extreme shock, and muttering, "It's just like a funeral!" It was a funeral — the burial not only of his career with that agency, but the burial of any pretence of decency in that troubled agency itself.

More recently, in the midst of my own battle with cancer, I had another reminder of the uncertainty in all of our lives. My youngest brother, Dave, came up for a visit from Buffalo because he was so concerned with my health crisis. Later he called me spontaneously, something he rarely did. A few days later I came home to a message that he had just died. He had been in perfect health and I kept exclaiming, "I don't believe it! This just is not happening. I can't believe it — I *won't* believe it!" For whatever reasons, I had accepted my health challenge with remarkably little denial but — perhaps because of that — my psyche refused to accept this one. For ten or fifteen minutes I went on babbling in this seemingly silly way, before I could even begin to ask relevant questions and to accept the shocking reality that it had happened. I knew all about shock so a part of me knew exactly what I was doing, but another part was in such shock that I neither knew nor cared. I just had to exclaim over and over my total refusal to accept this new, traumatic reality.

Shock cushions even physical pain so much that often accident victims are seen walking around the scene of an accident, when later they are found to have broken legs and other serious physical injuries. In the same way, our mind fastens on some interrupted task that is quite irrelevant now, but we are unable to take in the implications of the change. A friend of mine was driving a car hit by a train, and she and the car were carried far down the tracks. Pinned in her car, she was helped by a stranger who reached through her broken windshield to hold her hand till help could release her. She kept saying, "I have to go and make a phone call. I'll be late to the school."

Shock gives us the ability to worry about fussy details, or frees us to think heroically of others. Victims in airline accidents sometimes give help for hours to other victims, unaware of their own serious injuries. When subjected to a brutal firing, my first thought for days was to cushion the blow as much as possible for all others who would be affected by it. People who think of others when they themselves are deeply afflicted are acting heroically, for they wouldn't do it if they weren't strongly conditioned to think and act unselfishly. But shock helps them carry it out, by protecting them from the full impact they will feel later.

Physical shock lasts a matter of hours, but the psychological shock period for a major trauma goes on for weeks. There is a good way to tell when you are at the end of shock and the beginning of full grief: Shock is over when you wake up in the morning knowing it is all real, and not having to tell yourself again that the new horror is no nightmare. Having to face it anew each time you wake is one of the nastier parts of the shock period. It is an incentive to get on with your grief. There comes a time when our minds and souls would rather live with the pain continuously than have to face the bitter discovery one more time when we wake up that our previous world is gone forever.

Helping Ourselves

> Do not look forward to the changes and chances of this life in fear; rather look to them with full hope that, as they arise, God, whose you are, will deliver you out of them. Either He will shield you from suffering, or He will give you unfailing strength to bear it. Be at peace then, and put aside all anxious thoughts and imaginations.
>
> — FRANCIS DE SALES

There are a lot of adjustments to make to the loss we have experienced, and we need to make them moderately and sensibly, using every reasonable support life, our friends, and our family have to offer. Many of the things that help us most in this period help us again in grief. But here are some of the things other sufferers have discovered they could do to help them through the raw days of shock:

- Accept that you are human
- Don't take on unnecessary burdens
- Structure your time
- Begin by accepting the problem as an opportunity
- Moderate your expectations of friends

Accept That You Are Human

During the shock period we become objects of pity, and we get as much attention as we ever will. Allow yourself to be human. Don't be ashamed of feeling weak. It's a sign of stupidity, not strength, to walk around when a doctor is operating on you. A major trauma is like a serious operation. Treat yourself gently, as you would during and after major surgery. Allow yourself to express your pain and weakness.

Many people apologize for crying during the shock of a major trauma. Be glad for tears — they are cleansing and healthy. Tears are a gift God gives us to cleanse away some of the poisonous anger and anguish trauma brings. An old upper-class prescription for getting over a broken romance used to be a tour of the European continent. That had its pros and cons, but it did provide a break from continued reminders and pressures. Compassionate leave from workplaces or excused absences from scheduled student exams recognize the need to be gentle to those immersed in a fresh trauma.

Don't Take On Unnecessary Burdens

Don't go after hard experiences if they're not necessary. Plan a routine that includes treats that are most healing for you. If you get help from reading, pick out some of your favorite kinds of books. However, you may find it hard to concentrate, or that your tastes have changed. My sister who is a passionate reader could not read at first after the death of her child. Many people who normally love reading report that during shock they cannot take in the printed page. Their eyes see and rote read the individual words, but the concentration needed to absorb and comprehend the content eludes them. Don't worry if that happens to you — it is normal, and it will pass.

If you're a phone jockey, phone friends. If you get help from conferences, go to some. And if, as with reading for some people, the things that are usually fun don't work at all, don't worry about it and don't pressure yourself to squeeze pleasure out of places where it can't currently be found. Nothing will be "fun" in the usual sense during shock; but, if you keep experimenting, you will find some activities, new or old, which relieve some of the concentrated pain and anguish, first for a few moments, later, for longer.

If you feel you cannot take anything more *in*, try some activities that will help get some of your emotions *out*: writing, painting, music, crafts. One friend of mine was able to get through her father's funeral because she had spent the preceding two days writing the funeral service and crying buckets in private. The unexpected side benefit was that she was present enough that she could listen with pleasure to stories about her father from his friends. By the time the funeral arrived, she felt as though she had walked through the dark tunnel of shock and could see a small light at the other end.

If your trauma is bereavement, there may be certain places or experiences you should simply spare yourself for awhile. Associations are powerful, and we need to accept their power. If you do best with quiet, isolate yourself, but be careful how far you go with that, because all of us need some outside stimulation in times of trauma, or we can sink into depression. In fact, monitor anything you try, and adapt your program to what works for you at the time, in your present situation.

This is not the time to take on some task you have been dreading. Most people cannot even enjoy usually pleasurable activities when in fresh shock. A gourmet may lose his appetite. A singer may not be able to sing. Don't worry about these aberrations — they will pass. Let up on yourself, and trust God that this time will pass.

Structure Your Time

Whether your shock is the death of a mate, a miscarriage, the loss of a job, a crippling disease, or something else, it helps to structure your time. Any trauma disrupts our normal routines and puts an aching void in our lives. When my sister lost her two-year-old child, she still had a younger baby, but the diaper load was dramatically reduced. She found herself throwing other clothes in the diaper pail, to fill the tragically diminished load and dim the reality of the loss in her workload as well as in her heart. We need to establish new routines to look forward to and to supersede those that make our hearts ache with the reality of what is no more. My sister shifted her routine to increase her correspondence with me and spend more time with her other children.

Once again, don't try to make yourself do what is most painful, but pick out what fits for you best, here and now. It may be starting each day with a short prayer and then a morning walk. It may be fifteen minutes of aerobic exercises and a regular phone call with one very supportive friend. It may be taking responsibility for one or two daily household needs. It may be writing two letters to sympathetic friends. It could be all of these or a score of others. Playing the piano helps me, but if I try to do it too long when I am in deep shock or grief, my mind is free to harp on the aching wound, so I find that a short session on the piano is usually best.

Besides structuring your time positively, you can help yourself by planning healing activities that fit your particular personality and loves. Think about what heals you, and use it now, when you most need it. If you find travel is a balm, plan a trip for yourself. If restaurant evenings are a big treat for you, plan some with people you value. One friend I know finds that a complete new hairdo and outfit makes her feel positively rejuvenated. Another finds that jogging and a trip to the gym revitalizes her. Plan such things into those long months of grief. They won't take away the pain, but they will assist you in getting through the time with less anguish, until all the things you are learning have helped you to build a new life beyond it.

There is no right routine for everyone, nor will the routine be the same for you at different times. What matters is to find a structured routine that absorbs some of each day: something that you can wake up to in the morning with at least a little pleasure. The day is no longer just another day without what we have lost, but also a day in which we will be doing something useful or consoling or familiar or valuable to us and/or others. Often, volunteer work in a stimulating, but not too demanding, setting can help one through this period, but for others it is too much stress. Don't expect yourself to light on the right direction early, or to find it stable, during shock. Shock is a preliminary period — a time for experimenting with how to fill our changing grasp of the new, hard reality. Don't let anyone tell you that what worked for them is a must for you. The only thing that is a must for you is to find a way to structure each day that begins to infuse rhythm and meaning back into your life.

All of us have to go through the "Why Mes" and the "If Onlys" as part of the learning process. So, if there is anything you need to learn to avoid a repetition, learn it. But move as quickly as you can into *accepting the reality of what has happened*. Begin to realize, tragic as it may be, that reality is part of your life now, and so part of your life's opportunity. You can't accept the new reality all at once, but each gentle step you take reduces the resentment toward others and the guilt toward yourself, which can engulf and destroy you. Incredible as it sounds, you can emerge a better, stronger person from this agonizing experience.

In his remarkable book, *Flying Without Wings*, Arnold Beisser describes what it was like for him, at the age of twenty-five, to face becoming disabled. An accident forced him to leave forever a world where he had been a tournament tennis champion and able-bodied doctor, and become a quadriplegic who had to spend half of each day in an iron lung. Of course he had to overcome denial. How many incentives there were to retreat into a dream world instead of accepting the overwhelming challenges ahead of him! Beisser's spirit led him gradually toward a richly fulfilled life that fully integrated the new reality, but not before he struggled through the nightmare of shock and denial, followed by the long tunnel of grief.

Arnold Beisser writes eloquently of the eventual result of this quality of accepting problems as opportunities:

> When I stopped struggling, working to change, and found means of accepting what I had already become, I discovered that that changed me. Rather than feeling disabled and inadequate as I anticipated I would, I felt whole again. I experienced a sense of well being and fullness I had not known before. I felt at one not only with myself, but also with the universe.
>
> This was not change that had been wrought by struggle, work, and effort, but rather by learning how not to struggle, how to give in, to stand aside and let truth emerge. It was not the tragic truth I expected at all.
>
> When I allowed myself to face conditions that seemed intolerable

and experiences that seemed unthinkable, in their reality they changed. They changed from what seemed to be horrible to something only acceptable at first, then both interesting and fulfilling. I learned that to make a place for myself in the world, it was not always necessary to struggle, for I had a place already within me.

Beisser did not arrive at this state quickly, and I am not suggesting that such an advanced stage of acceptance is possible in the shock stage. But, we can set our sails in that direction and know that the spirit of what Beisser is saying is true. We do have to go through denial, anguish, and anger, but in the end any problem can become an opportunity.

Etty Hillesum was a young Dutch Jewish woman who died in Auschwitz. In her book, An Interrupted Life, she has expressed this point eloquently: "I now realize, God, how much You have given me: so much that was beautiful, and so much that was hard to bear. Yet whenever I showed myself ready to bear it, *the hard was directly transformed into the beautiful.*" That's the key: acceptance transforms the hard into the beautiful.

For out of the horrors of the Holocaust arose heroes of the spirit — Etty Hillesum, Anne Frank, Eli Weisel, Raoul Wallenburg, and so many others — heroes whose true greatness could not have shone without that historic blasphemy. If there are opportunities even in the Holocaust, surely there are opportunities in the burdens each of us are called to bear.

Moderate Your Expectations of Friends

One final caution to those entering shock from their first major trauma — try not to expect too much from friends. If you lower your expectations, you will not add bitter disappointment to the grief you are already struggling to accept. Indulge yourself when you have a choice, yes, but don't expect others to indulge you. For all the reasons stated in our opening chapter, most people in our culture are ill-equipped to offer the type of support described in this book, which is so needed by friends in trauma. They are terrified by the depths of your trauma and by their own sense of incapacity to respond adequately. Either they fear facing the reality that you, a good and careful person, are suffering deeply, indicating that they might one day have to suffer too; or they fear saying or doing the wrong thing, something that will wound instead of help you.

Either way, many of them will withdraw just when you need them most, or worse still, will blame you in some way for this tragedy. I have been helped enormously in accepting this erosion of support when it is most needed by resolving that I would learn from it, and apply the knowledge to help all others in trauma. In this way, I am hoping that the disappointments I have experienced from friends disappearing will be less likely to happen to others. This is the gift of finding meaning or significance in our traumas, and is one of the greatest gifts of all. It is out of that gift that this book has been born, and is why I have devoted years to calling, writing, and supporting friends going through all kinds of trauma. You too can become an expert in trauma, filling some of the great needs all around you. But you can't do it if you get bogged down in bitterness over the friends that aren't there for you. Learn lightly from them what not to do, celebrate and emulate the beautiful responses from those who are there, and remember that even this is not constant. Sometimes a friend can't deal with one particular crisis — perhaps only because it hits too close to one of his or her own traumas or fears — but they may be there for you next time.

Whatever challenges your period of shock holds, know that you can bear whatever you have to, that this too will pass, and that for every hour you bear, you have become a stronger person, one of those who prove to the world that we can survive trauma triumphantly. But the path of any triumph is grungy and filled with potholes — tread it faithfully and patiently.

Helping Others

At the times when you cannot see God, there is still the opportunity to use this sacred possibility: to *show* God; there may be times when you cannot *find* help, but there is no time when you cannot *give* help.

— GEORGE MERRIAM in *Daily Strength for Daily Needs*

There are four basic rules that will help you when someone you love is suffering from a trauma:

- Do something, not nothing
- You do the reaching
- Meet the principal victim's needs, not your own
- Show respect: don't blame the victim

Do Something, Not Nothing

There are so many reasons for doing nothing when someone we know is struck with trauma. First of all, there is just plain inertia. Our lives are full, and it is a lot easier just not to think about this unpleasant business, and let the rest of our own busy lives fill our time. Then soon, it becomes embarrassingly late, and so we avoid our friend and the issue by keeping even busier. Eventually, we shrug our shoulders and rationalize, "I wasn't really that close to Joe, and he's active in his church. His minister can help him deal with this better than I can. In the summer, when he's over all this, I'll call him up and we'll go out again for tennis. He can't expect anything more."

Secondly, there is the fear of doing something wrong when we feel unsure what is best to offer. We all feel in over our heads in trauma; no one likes to walk into a calculus exam when their last experience with math was failing it in sixth grade. There is also the fear of disturbing our own tenuous equilibrium — trauma is infectious, and if we face it with others, we have to face that it can happen to us too. A friend of mine who did overcome her fear and take me out to lunch kept repeating, "I can't understand how they could show so much disrespect to you!" Clearly, although she faced her fear and overcame it magnificently during that lunch, she was struggling with the awful thought that if I, with all my degrees and credentials, could be fired, it could happen to her or anyone. Others with less courage and the same fear simply avoided me and felt unable to face me, because facing me reminded them that job trauma could happen to them too.

Emil Fuchs, whose daughter was driven to suicide by Nazi oppression, wrote:

Do not, therefore, close your eyes before the sufferings of your neighbors. Do not fear that it will destroy your happiness if you live in sympathy with them. This indeed brings something like a shadow into your life, and at the first moment you feel you cannot endure it; so you try to forget it. No. Hold it fast; take it into your life. Bring it into touch with your own happiness and joy. All that is only superficial will vanish, but the real happiness of family, of art and song, of nature and friendship and devotion — all will grow and become more real until they become that holiness in which they are a part of God's presence in our lives.

So clumsy though you may feel, frightened though you may feel, reach out a helping hand to your friend in trauma. Be guided by empathy toward his or her feelings and you can't go far wrong. A letter, a call, a visit, flowers, a gift, a service — all these things lighten the sufferer's load and bond them to the community at a time when their ties to life itself seem shattered. Let your gesture reflect the personality of the recipient as much as possible. They may prefer a living plant to cut flowers or chocolate to other gifts. Let your gesture carry with it the promise of continued caring, but don't promise more than you intend to deliver. Empty promises of help that don't materialize add to the burden.

Many sufferers have described gestures that have touched them, and made them feel surrounded by a cocoon of love when they were numb with shock and could not fend for themselves. Homemade food is one of the commonest offerings, but also a very meaningful one. An uncle of mine was caught in a white-collar crime. Deeply ashamed, he could not eat the jail food. His wife filed for divorce, but his mother-in-law, my grandmother, stood behind him. Grandma cooked him her wonderful homemade food, and Uncle Jim was able to digest these gifts of love when he could not digest anything else.

You Do the Reaching

Don't burden the person in trauma with a vague "anything I can do to help" offer that means nothing, however well intended. Use your imagination and offer specific support. Send letters, make calls, deliver groceries, ask their children over for an outing. Grief is very enervating, and the effort to pick up the phone when you are depressed is enormous, let alone deciding who to call and what to dare to ask for, risking a rebuff. Even a phone machine may feel like a rejection. Compare this with an incoming call: "Barry, I've got two tickets to the game, and I know you're a fan, too. Can you come with me next Wednesday?"

When my mother was dying a long, slow death from Alzheimer's disease, our Friends Meeting became aware of how much this was restricting our activities. A Friend in the Meeting, not one I had been particularly close to, called and asked me to go to a rendition of one of the Choral Masses. I was touched by the invitation; we went and had a good visit, and I was able to take a break from the interminable state at home. But most importantly, I felt a tangible caring reaching out to me, and I felt a bond of love. In a later experience of family stress, we were surprised when two friends with professional skills insisted on coming in to give our house a cleaning.

On the subject of house cleaning, there is a funny, true story about Nancy and John Pocock, two great Quaker activists in our Friends Meeting. When John died of a malignant brain tumor, both the Catholics and the Communists wanted to express their support, the Catholics because John's brother was a bishop and the Communists because the Pococks had worked with them on a number of common causes for social justice. So the Catholics held a special mass for John's spirit while, at the same time, the Communists cleaned their house. It was a unique accidental collaboration for a unique couple, but it also represented two different but equally appropriate expressions of love and support.

Native people in Alkali Lake have found a beautiful way of expressing support to members turning their lives around from alcoholism. This amazing community has worked together to change from a state of one hundred percent alcoholism to ninety-five percent dry and clean. One of the keys is that the whole community works together: first, in making a person aware of their problem and getting them ready for treatment, and secondly, in supporting them through that major transition. So, when people return from residence in the thirty-day treatment program nearby, they find their house cleaned and painted, a symbol of their new life.

Even if your offer is rejected, the very reaching out has helped. The person in trauma has had the chance to make a choice, and chances are they appreciated the offer even if, for whatever reason, they didn't take you up on it. Reach out, not once, but repeatedly. But shape your reaching to the cues you get from the person towards whom you are reaching.

Meet the Principal Victim's Needs, Not Your Own

So many of these suggestions may seem obvious, yet few people under the stress of a real emergency remember all of them. The problem with a major trauma is that there is no one victim, as a rule. The closer a friend is to the person(s) at the center, the more likely they are to be deeply wounded by the trauma, too. As a result, the very people the sufferer would usually reach to for help are often buried in their own grief — for example, the whole range of relatives of a child killed in an accident. It takes heroic sensitivity for the bereaved parents to focus on the needs of a frightened, grieving sibling.

But even friends of the family can be surprisingly caught up in their own needs. They want to be reassured by the family that it is really all right, and they find it frightening to hear over and over again of the shock and grief and loss. They quickly begin to meet their own needs for reassurance and a sense of control by telling the family, "Don't cry — stiff upper lip does it. She's better off, you know, and you have to go on for the sake of the others." Such messages begin to come through even in the early days of shock, and they certainly do not meet the normal, healthy needs of bereaved parents, or other shock victims.

Trauma is a chance to show that you are an emotional grownup. Practice every bit of empathy you have, and meet the needs of the people at the center. You'll find you grow from it, and amazingly enough, your own needs for reassurance are better met by this sensitivity than by panicky attempts to fit the victims into your program.

Show Respect: Don't Blame the Victim

All your actions should show absolute respect for the person(s) in the storm center. I frequently call them victims because there is no other single word for their role, yet everything you and they do should help them to transform the victim role into an active, triumphant one. Amazingly enough, whenever I have been visited with trauma, I find that for all the intended support, there is a lot of patronizing advice that comes with it. A lot of amateur doctors and psychiatrists think they know how you could have avoided this, and they are eager to tell you so. They even bring up faults or alleged faults that have nothing at all to do with your catastrophe. Your moment of vulnerability just seems to some people an ideal time to let you know things they have been meaning to get off their chest about how you can improve your life!

Of course, such well-meant advice is ill-timed and counter-productive. It is almost as if people know your defenses are too low to fight back, so they are getting in their advice while it is safe. Closely related are "Job's comforters," who blame the victim for her/his disaster. "I really think you should go to a psychiatrist," they suggest to someone attacked for their political views. Or, "If your diet had been healthier, perhaps you wouldn't have been eating at a hamburger stand and the accident wouldn't have happened." It's hard to say whether these kinds of non-sequiturs hurt more or less than relevant criticisms. Suffice it to say that blaming the victim is not a helpful strategy. Listening is, and we shall talk more about that in the next section, on helping people in the grief stage.

One of the best responses to suffering arising from trauma is Fra Giovanni's classic Christmas Letter of 1513:

I am your friend, and my love for you goes deep.
There is nothing I can give you which you have not;
But there is much, very much that, while I cannot give it, you can take.
No Heaven can come to us unless our hearts find rest in it today.
Take Heaven!

No peace lies in the future which is not hidden in this present little
  instant.
  Take Peace!
The gloom of the world is but a shadow.
Behind it, yet within our reach is JOY.
  There is radiance and glory in the darkness, could we but see;
  And to see, we have only to look. I beseech you to LOOK.
Life is so generous a giver, but we, judging its gifts by their covering,
Cast them aside as ugly, or heavy, or hard.
  Remove the covering, and you will find beneath it
  A living splendor, woven of love
  By wisdom, with power.
Welcome it, grasp it, and you touch the Angel's hand that brings it to
  you.
Everything we call a trial, a sorrow, or a duty:
Believe me, that angel's hand is there;
  The gift is there, and the wonder of an Overshadowing Presence.
Our joys too — be not content with them as joys.
  They too conceal diviner gifts.
Life is so full of meaning and of purpose, so full of beauty beneath its
  covering
  That you will find that earth but cloaks your heaven.
Courage then to claim it: that is all!
But courage you have; and the knowledge that we are pilgrims together,
  Wending through unknown country, home.
And so at this time I greet you,
  Not quite as the world sends greetings,
  But with profound esteem,
And with the prayer that for you,
  Now and forever,
  The Day breaks,
  And the shadows flee away.

You can help a friend in trauma. Do act, and choose your gestures with empathy and respect. Take the initiative yourself, and tune in to your friend's responses to find the best step to take next in your continued reaching out. A friend who can do all the things described here is a friend indeed. However much we may make mistakes, we need to keep trying. The spirit of faithful love shines through all the bumbling in the world, and is cherished for the pure gold that it is.

CHAPTER 3

Trouble Comes to Us All

Do not look forward to the changes and chances of this life in fear; rather look to them with full hope that, as they arise, God, whose you are, will deliver you out of them. Either He will shield you from suffering, or He will give you unfailing strength to bear it. Be at peace then, and put aside all anxious thoughts and imaginations.

— Francis de Sales

As with everyone else on this planet, my life has seen its share of trauma. In my case the most significant were two brutal job losses and two bouts with cancer. It may come as a surprise to learn that my deepest wounds were the firings and not the cancer. In fact, often I tell people that after facing these firings — and all the learning and spiritual growth inherent in recovering from them — facing cancer was a walk in the park. At least no one was blaming me for getting fired from life! For years I've been trying to help people learn that job traumas are just as serious, if not more serious, than many other traumas since they call our whole self-image and worth as a person into question. These incidents are not accidents; they are triggered by enemies we may not even have known that we had, not simple bad luck. This aspect makes it a challenge to trust and to work with people again.

Cancer, too, has been seen as an enemy, but an enemy within – our own bodies turn on us and become malignant. There are many views of cancer in various cultures. In our increasingly poisoned environment many see can-cer as a mark of humanity's lack of harmony with our environment, Mother Earth. Others see cancer as a sign that we are not living in harmony with ourselves – that something is out of balance in our lives. Whatever view one takes of it, and whatever the outcome, survival or remission or death, the battle with cancer is an increasingly common one.

Loss of Innocence

> If thou suffer injustice, console thyself; the true unhappiness is in doing it.
>
> — DEMOCRITUS

My first and most traumatic job loss was from the Bail-Out Program based in Old City Hall. The agency helped low-income people raise bail rather than remain in jail awaiting trial. Although I had founded the agency, I had been dismissed with no thanks, no acknowledgment of my four years of arduous pioneer service, and no recognition of my strengths. Basically, I was fired by my own board over differing visions of the program. I was amazed to discover that I could not ride or walk past that building without great pain. So much joy had occurred there, so much love had been given and received, and then so much cruelty in the months of anguish that ended that beautiful experience. Whenever I saw Old City Hall, all those feelings were wrapped together, but coated deeply with the anguish. So, for a while, I learned to avoid passing it, and helped myself by that avoidance to swim through the tidal waves of the deepest grief.

But in the long run, we need to face our nemeses, and so gradually I learned to pass the building, and was delighted when I felt less and less pain in the passing. Then one Christmas, the mother of three young men I had helped, who worked for a professional photographer and had herself learned some of those skills, gave me a very special gift: a beautiful photo-graph of Old City Hall. Touched by her thoughtfulness, and by the memo-ries of the love we had shared when I worked there, I found the pain had been exorcised. The picture now occupies a prominent place on our buffet, and symbolizes for me the love and creativity of those four years, as well as the ability God gives us to transcend grief and grow through and beyond it. That picture now brings me nothing but joy and pride when I look at it, but it would have been folly to try to rub my face in it when the pain was fresh and grief was so incomplete.

One of the most helpful comments made to me during this trauma was by my closest friend at the time. She told me with absolute clarity, "You are going to feel even worse, and this will go on for a year, but in the end you are going to come through this and do much more significant things than you ever did." The first part of that may not have sounded like cheering input, but it prepared me better than anything else did for the long, bitter year ahead. As month after month of grief contradicted my natural optimism, I remembered both halves of her prophecy. I was better able to accept the grief, and I clung to the positive prophecy shining at the end of it, which also proved to be true.

Within that year I found myself at a gathering where an acquaintance was being honored for her years of service. At the time, I was still grieving deeply for that job loss. For years afterwards, going to farewells where other people were being honored, often for service less total or long than mine had been, brought up these painful wounds. On this occasion, the wounds were still bleeding. The helplessness of grief kept me in my seat for a few moments. Then it occurred to me that I *could leave*. The first key in avoiding needless injury is to recognize we have choices and to evaluate those choices as objectively as we can. So when it dawned on me that I didn't have to be there, I began to ask myself questions. Was it cowardly of me to leave? Would I regret not having confronted my vulnerable situation head-on? Would it bother the person being honored, or anyone else, if I quietly left?

As I explored each of these questions I gained an increasing sense of power. I realized that having the courage to leave a situation that was needlessly reopening a fresh wound was strong, not weak. I was not sure I would have no regrets, but the more I listened to my inner self, the more sure I was that this was the best choice for me, and I would be able to answer any second thoughts I had about it afterwards. A major factor in my answers to these two questions was that I was not close to the person being honored, there were many persons there who were, and neither she nor anyone else would notice or care if I left quietly. Her receiving proper recognition did not depend at all on me, so my staying would weaken me, and not strengthen her at all. As these things became clear to me, I quietly got up and left. I felt good about that choice then, and I have been proud of it ever since. It taught me a new lesson in asserting my own needs, and in not suffering unnecessary pain just to prove I can do it. I *know* I can endure pain, but I am also strong enough not to wallow in it deliberately when my suffering serves no good purpose.

After this first great trauma, my husband encouraged me to think of something I would like to do just for myself that would celebrate and affirm my passage through that hard, dark time. We rarely ask ourselves what we would most like to do just for ourselves, but when I did, I realized it was a trip to visit a particular couple. Their home included a fruit orchard in southern California with fresh oranges to pick for breakfast year round. But the real attractions were John and Hanne themselves. John was the most wonderful chamber music player I had ever shared music with, and Hanne had written the most deeply spiritual support letters to me during that period. Going to their home was all I dreamed of and more. That treat did more than affirm my healing; it reminded me that we could use affirmative experiences to help heal deep wounds, so that we fear future traumas less.

One friend who helped me a great deal was a dear friend who lived thousands of miles away, but who wrote me of her own loss of innocence, and understood both the beauty and the bitterness of mine. Her letter identified so totally with my suffering it was as if she shared it all with me. The mystery I felt through it was that, had she not had her own innocence brutally ripped from her, she would not have been able to reach me in my despair. I, in turn, found my loss of innocence enabled me to reach out in compassion to people in pain in ways I had never before dreamed possible.

Another friend ran away from me during my first firing. We had been very close and her friendship meant so much to me, I ached for her support but she never called and never communicated. A couple of years later I approached her and we made our peace over that episode. She actually apologized and took responsibility for her absence, acknowledging she was just too scared and overwhelmed by the whole situation to do anything but run away. Seven years later when a similar event erupted in my life, she was one of the early ones to call and set a lunch, and she said gladly, "I am *not* going to blow this one this time!" Nor did she. We can grow, and we can help our friends grow, in this life call to give and receive first aid in times of trauma.

Several weeks after the firing, my youngest daughter asked me, "Mom, have you forgiven the Board?" What a question, and what a moment of truth! I tried very hard to examine myself and answer truthfully. I thought of my refusal to entertain hatred or wishes of harm, and of my absolute will to forgiveness. After a moment, with some hesitation, I replied, "Yes, Joy, I have forgiven them."

But although I had sincerely tried to be honest, the answer did not sit well. I knew, as I thought about it, that I had not *arrived* at forgiveness. Joy's question stimulated a self-searching, which led me to a new understanding that I shared with her a few days later. "Remember when you asked me if I had forgiven the Board, and I said I had? Well, I've been thinking about that, and I think there is more to it than that. Some wrongs are so big and so deep and so unrecognized by the world that it may take our whole lives to work on forgiveness. But we can make the commitment to the path to forgiveness, and what I meant is that I have made that commitment. Forgiveness is a process, a commitment to a process. So what I should have said is, 'I am on the path of forgiveness.'"

About a year after the firing I had arrived at the point of being able to say whimsically, "I have finally come to the conclusion that I don't know now and probably never will understand what God means by this chapter in my life. But I have also concluded that there is a meaning, that God knows what it is, and that I don't need to." That was my particular discovery of peace with God.

Life's Hard Lessons

No life is so hard that you can't make it easier by the way you take it.

— Ellen Glasgow

In my own job losses, I learned from the first experience what to avoid in the second. Having no office downtown, no place to *be* made me feel very much a wanderer and unwanted. So in my more recent experience I planned my days carefully to avoid interim periods between downtown meetings when I would have nowhere to be. I found taking long walks filled in some of the cracks and benefited my health. I learned to turn down invitations, however well meant, that would take me downtown without a coordinated series of reasons for being there.

I applied my own advice on volunteering after my second job loss from the Half-Way Society; an organization set up to help ex-prisoners reintegrate into the community. In a bitter and ironic twist of fate I was fired from that job for believing that we should set a good example and hire ex-prisoners at the society itself.

Toronto had a dynamic city councilor, Jack Layton, now the national leader of the New Democratic Party (NDP), whose energy for good causes and individual needs abounded in many directions (and still does). I had said for some years that if ever I had free time, I would love to volunteer in his office. So when my being suspended with pay led to just such a period, I did exactly that. Being part of Jack's amazing office one or two days a week gave me positive experiences to take the bitter taste of my own troubles out of my mouth. I realized that I had been trying to plant healthy seeds in bad soil and that the Society had pathological organizational problems. Working in a healthy organization helped me deal with the continuing horrors of my own situation. It also reminded me of my own worth at a time when many people were dumping on me, and it structured my time, giving me a positive place to be and people to work with, contrasting well with the craziness I had just left.

I also encountered lots of examples of what *not* to do for someone in trauma. One loyal and supportive employee chose the day after my firing to tell me that if only I would dress better, things would go better in my life. Casual as my dress style is, it had nothing to do with my firings over social issues, and her remark, coming from someone whose loyalty and understanding I had come to depend upon, and when I was so vulnerable, felt like a kick when I was already down.

But it is far easier to blame friends, particularly those we admire, when they lash out with violent emotions, and such blaming handicaps them in their search for freedom from those very emotions. When I told a dear friend how I was made ill the first time I had to be in a room with someone who had betrayed me deeply, he accused me of un-Christian feelings and of unhealthy emotions. I accepted his criticism, and it slowed down my healing. Now years later, I know that nothing could have been more natural than that strong reaction. I needed to have it accepted as normal, so I could begin to get through it, on the way to letting it go.

Another friend cut me off when I was describing the behavior of an opponent who had denied me access to my personal belongings in a way that felt very cruel to me. My friend started giving me all the good reasons why this might have been done, till I felt that any anger I had was wholly unacceptable in her eyes. When I tried to tell her that I needed to have my anger accepted, she became angry with me for trying to advise her how to help me. Neither of us at that moment was able to accept fully the other's emotions.

The position of one of my friends was very satisfying, however. More than a year after I had been thrown out of my job, she refused to apply for it. But with difficulty, I learned also to accept those who felt they could go on working there under the new regime.

In the fall of 2000, our daughter Joy was disappointed that Trent University, where she had attended as an undergraduate, and where many of her closest friends still lived, did not pursue a particular fellowship option with her which might have enabled her to teach there. She spoke of it as a lost dream, but with her usual wisdom realized that while she needed to grieve this disappointment, she needed to not get hooked on the "lost dream" imagery.

I wrote her in response that I had learned how important it was not to wallow in angry talk to myself. I told her of my finding out that several of my former antagonists in my last job rejection were doing very well indeed within their large organization. I had spent some time bemoaning the fact that all three of them were heads of significant areas, while all three had behaved with extreme cruelty to me personally. Then I realized this was not productive, and I began saying instead, "They are the kind of people who fit that organization, which is sad for it. I have been given the gift of working in better places like ICOPA, Focus, and Rittenhouse, where my gifts can find richer fulfillment." I stopped being bitter and regurgitating my own bile, and got back on the positive.

So I advised Joy not to focus on any mantra here whose repetition could potentially lock her into grief and bitterness, which was not her way in any case. I reminded her that with all her gifts some wonderful path was unfolding now which she could not anticipate. And, being Joy, she followed that path quickly, not without sorrow for the lost dream, but without bitterness and without keeping her face turned to the past.

When I had to face my cruelest opponents and a critical press at an inquest – part of the fall-out from my second firing — I prayed as earnestly as I ever have, simply to live love all week long. Such a prayer, not for victory for our side, nor even for vindication, but simply to be love, is a prayer that will always be answered. I lived that week, not without pain, but in a glow of spiritual power that shines in my life still today. I know that some of what people today see in me is the glow that came from that and other struggles to surrender antagonism and live love in some of life's toughest challenges.

Planning some treats for myself also helped me get over grief. During that difficult inquest, I promised myself that if it were very harsh, I would take a trip somewhere just to celebrate the end of a hard period, and give myself a break. The best moment I had in a recent trauma was when my son asked me to accompany him to a conference I had wanted to go to all my life, and I suddenly realized that precisely because of this trauma, I could finally indulge myself. I know religious conferences are one of my most healing experiences, so I gave myself this healing opportunity. I also planned a series of short trips, spacing them over the first hard months of my grief period.

After one of my job traumas, I had an interesting and unexpected experience. A white traffic policeman shot and wounded a 16-year-old black youth for a fairly flagrant traffic violation. The community was up in arms about the shooting, and the policeman was suspended with pay, and charged with criminal negligence.

Normally my identification would have been entirely with the boy, his family, and the black community. It still mostly was. But when I read of the suspension with pay of this policeman with a ten-year record of service, something clicked. I knew the utter dedication I had given to my job, and I too was suspended with pay. I knew experientially just how much suffering and humiliation there was for him in that condition. Of course I hadn't shot anyone, and of course I believed my suspension to be wholly unjust, but that very unjust suffering enabled me to understand, as I had never understood before, all the humiliation, all the helplessness of being suspended with pay.

I didn't agree any more than I had before with his use of a gun on an unarmed youngster. But I knew with my whole soul what his anguish felt like, and my heart went out to him. I never could have felt that way without having had such a similar experience. So we need to learn empathy ourselves, while accepting graciously each gift of empathy from others. Give up the temptation to yearn for more.

Victory or Defeat?

> As Henry van Dyke wrote, "Some kinds of defeat are better than victory." …even when the world tells you that you are defeated, you can take pride in living daringly, dangerously, and positively for the betterment of others.
> — RUTH MORRIS, *Stories of Transformative Justice*

Each year for many years, we have written a Christmas letter to many friends and shared it with some acquaintances. In it we sum up the lives of our children and the main events of our year. But we also begin with some quotation that sums up my main spiritual challenge or learning for the year, and somewhere in the letter, usually at the end, talk about the spiritual dimensions of the year. We talk about our creative failures as well as our successes. No doubt our open airing of these deep topics puts off some people. But each year some people respond with warmth on the same level of deep spiritual sharing. I have noticed that the more I have shared the deep pain and profound growing, the more our Christmas mail returns rich sharing letters as well. As I was writing this, a work colleague I have valued phoned to share how much our opening quote for the year spoke to events in her life about which I had known nothing. This kind of risking in love is a foundation for supporting one another through all the griefs all of us bear. For until we learn to talk more deeply about these common human challenges, each of us feels more isolated, as if we alone were wandering in the desert of our own private traumas.

Just as our Christmas letter is an example of how general letters can establish more of a common basis for supporting one another in trauma, personal letters to a sufferer can be tremendously healing. Here is one support letter I received after one firing:

> I am so sorry for the horror show you have been put through — you of all people. I think of you as the Julia Child of these particular good works!
>
> This Earth School certainly knows how to give lessons! Sometimes I do just want to get off altogether — then I wonder if the spirit world isn't full of young souls creating as much trouble there as here — and so I hang in longer. What a hollow victory for those egos living in illusion! How little they gain by such separating actions! Murderers of souls, like murderers of bodies, need our prayers — and I send them to them — all the while I hold you in love and admiration for the surfacing from it all that you are doing with grace. I know the next thing on your journey will turn up — have faith and till your garden...
>
> ...As little 8-year-old Tegan said recently, "I am sad that my Dad died, cause I miss him, but I am happy too cause I know he is still around and I can talk to him — you can't break love, you know, you can't break love."
>
> You are in my circle of healing,
>
> — LS

There were so many healing messages in that letter. First it affirmed my value. Secondly, it identified my suffering as part of a vast company of suffering, not an isolating experience. Third, it recognized the despair all of us feel at times, and validated my sense of outrage and wrong. Fourth, it showed me the road of pitying my opponents for their blindness, as a part of forgiving them for the cruelty that had come from it. Finally, it sent waves of love across the miles so strong I could almost feel their warmth penetrating my whole body and soul.

Friends can also help grievers discover that though they feel alone; theirs is a common path, trodden by people through the ages. One friend sent me a copy of Kipling's "If" and the poem both reminded me of her continued admiration for me when I felt so denigrated, and of the universal community of suffering:

If you can keep your head when all about you
    Are losing theirs and blaming it on you;
If you can trust yourself when all men doubt you,
    But make allowance for their doubting too;
If you can wait and not be tired by waiting,
    Or, being lied about, don't deal in lies,
Or, being hated, don't give way to hating,
    And yet don't look too good, nor talk too wise;

If you can dream — and not make dreams your master;
    If you can think — and not make thoughts your aim,
If you can meet with triumph and disaster
    And treat those two impostors just the same;
If you can bear to hear the truth you've spoken
    Twisted by knaves to make a trap for fools,
Or watch the things you gave your life to broken,
    And stoop and build 'em up with wornout tools:
. . . If you can fill the unforgiving minute
    With sixty seconds' worth of distance run—
Yours is the Earth and everything that's in it,
    And — which is more — you'll be a Man, my son!

The male orientation notwithstanding, there is a lot of power in that old poem, with its recognition of the twinning of triumph and disaster, and the fact that both are false gods, worshipped instead of growth, love, and discovery on our journeys. The emphasis on accepting the distortions of the world, and going on to rebuild with whatever we have left is also very healing to one bruised by recent slanders, abuse, and wanton destruction. Disheartening as it is to know that things like this have happened for many decades, there is also something consoling in knowing we are not isolated in being picked on by the world, and that writers and achievers as famous as Kipling have experienced them too.

What despair there is in working hard for good results only to find all your work misunderstood or washed away. The famous monk Thomas Merton received a letter from Jim Douglass, a young Canadian peace activist, about his sense of discouragement in the struggle to give his life toward peace, the lack of understanding and response. Merton's letter of response is full of wisdom so profound I get different tones from the prism of truths in it each time I read it:

Dear Jim,

Do not depend on the hope of results. When you are doing the kind of work you have taken on, essentially an apostolic work, you may have to face the fact that your work will be apparently worthless and even achieve no result at all, if not perhaps results opposite to what you expect. As you get used to this idea, you start more and more to concentrate not on the results but on the value, the rightness, the truth of the work itself. And there too a great deal has to be gone through, as gradually you struggle less and less for an idea, and more and more and more for specific people... In the end, it is the reality of personal relationships that saves everything.

You are fed up with words, and I don't blame you. I am nauseated by them sometimes... Your system is complaining of too much verbalizing and it is right. ...The big results are not in your hands or mine, but they suddenly happen, and we can share in them; but there is no point in building our lives on this personal satisfaction, which may be denied us and which after all is not that important.

The next step in the process is for you to see that your own thinking about what you are doing is crucially important. You are probably striving to build yourself an identity in your work, out of your work, and your witness. You are using it, so to speak, to protect yourself against nothingness, annihilation. That is not the right use of your work. All the good that you will do will come not from you but from the fact that you have allowed yourself, in the obedience of faith, to be used by God's love. Think of this more and gradually you will be free from the need to prove yourself, and you can be more open to the power that will work through you without your knowing it . . .

The real hope, then, is not in something we think we can do, but in God who is making something good out of it in some way we cannot see. If we can do His will, we will be helping in this process. But we will not necessarily know all about it beforehand... Enough of this... it is at least a gesture... I will keep you in my prayers...

This letter, which has been passed from hand to hand by social activists like a thermos of precious water in a desert, speaks to that trite concept of "burnout" on a profound level. It stresses the value of *process* over *results*. There was an attender in our Friends Meeting who was controversial, and some felt that if we could just hang on until her therapy settled her down, all would be well. I believed that we should not have a goal of surviving till she is more healed, but that we needed to learn to value the process of healing itself. We needed to struggle along with her as she was, with all of us growing with her in learning new ways to include the marginalized.

Merton's letter also mentions the importance of people, and of relationships. I do get tired of people saying that an organization is more important than the people it continues to hurt, or the processes it continues to violate, or even the mission it has lost sight of. Merton reminds us that it may not be granted to us to see results in our lifetime, and even less so to be credited with our part in the struggle.

Not long after I had been booted out of my second significant justice system job, a fairly high ranking corrections official called to ask if she could use my name as a reference for a promotion. I was amazed that she would think that after all I had been through, my name and reference could help her. Her belief in the ongoing validity of my work in the field, and the value of my name even to highly placed corrections officials did much to reassure me that all the attacks I had suffered could not destroy my solid contributions. Incidentally, she got the job!

Quakers tell a true story about Stephen Grellet, a Quaker who felt called to preach a sermon whilst standing in the midst of a wild clearing in the woods of early Pennsylvania. Grellet tried his best to curb this call — it was absurd to stand there and hold forth to the trees and empty sky! But something kept stirring within him, and being an extraordinarily tuned-in person, he conceded to the Hound of Heaven, opened his voice, and gave forth a long and eloquent sermon. Relieved at having done what he felt called to do, he went his way and forgot about it.

Years later he met a man in England who was converting many people to Quakerism and living an inspired life of faith. In talking together, the two men discovered that this great preacher had been a woodsman in the trees in Pennsylvania that day, and had been so moved by the words Grellet preached to the seemingly empty air that he had gone away a completely changed man! The story illustrates dramatically how little it is given to us to know when our words truly have fallen on deaf ears, and when God is waiting for God's own time to use them for divine purposes.

My sister and her husband took in teenage foster children for awhile. One of them, John, was a difficult boy and they seemed to make no headway. Finally he was arrested for something, and they lost track of him, feeling they had failed. Some years later John came back, and said to them, "I know you thought you never reached me, *but you did*. I felt love from you as I had never felt it before. I could not turn myself around right away, but eventually, I did, and now I have a home, a job, and a family. I have you to thank for all that." As Jesus found out when he healed ten lepers, only one returned to give thanks. John's remembering to do so reminds us that all our acts of love that appear to us to bring only traumatic rejection may have positive consequences that only appear to us years later, if at all.

In helping friends through trauma it is important to remember that the love you send is the gift, and the particular form is the wrapping paper: pretty, but not the core. The work itself, as Merton points out, is what counts, not your own reward for it or identity with the work. "All the good that you will do will come not from you but from the fact that you have allowed yourself, in the obedience of faith, to be used by God's love."

CHAPTER 4

Grief: Walking That Lonesome Valley

I began what I think of as the long journey through the dark
tunnel of grief, feeling that in time there would be light.
— MOTHER OF TEENAGED SUICIDE VICTIM

GRIEF IS LIKE A LONG, SLOW, indefinite sentence. It goes on and on,
and again and again the direct sufferer and those living through it
with him or her cry, "When will it ever end?" As the quote above says, it is
like a dark tunnel, and part of its pain is our inability to control it. Grief is
partly about losing control, losing something we want desperately and can
no longer have.

Grief will last a long time, even well past the time that you have reached
acceptance and begun to heal. One friend of mine tells me that, even ten
years afterwards, she feels waves of grief sometimes watching grandfathers
play with their grandchildren because her father died when her first child
was only six months old and never got much of a chance to be a grandfather. Watching other grandfathers reminds her of what her own children are
missing — the opportunity to get to know her wonderful father.

But although we cannot control the world outside us, we can learn to
handle our own response so that the tunnel brings us closer to the person
we are meant to become. All the preparation in the world doesn't stop the
pain; it just trains you in how to bear it. Grief is like labor pains. It helped
me enormously when I caught on to the similarity. Grief, like labor, comes
in waves of rising pain that threaten to overwhelm you. As you go into each

one, there is a moment of near panic, because you *know* how much pain is ahead, and you wonder if you can bear it, and if it ever will end. But experience tells you that you *can* bear it. Natural childbirth and other methods train us to relax and accept pain, breathing deeply into it, and knowing it will pass. I do the same with my regular waves of grief pain. They are part of our gifts too, and we must learn to bear them. Each one we bear leaves us stronger than we were before.

Walking the Lonely Road

> I know death is only a change of form. That the Being does not cease. As a consequence, I feel no fear about my own death or another's, and I don't think of death as having ended the Beingness of loved ones. Rather, I *think* of my personal loss, and I *feel* my personal loss, while sustaining ongoing contact in my Being — in Higher Self — with loved ones. And I *am at peace, while my feelings run the gamut of pain to happiness.*
>   — MIRIAMNE PAULUS, personal sharing, 1987

Grief is in many ways the longest, hardest part of the process of enduring and growing through trauma. Shock has worn us out, and friends are worn out and weary of us, and suddenly we find ourselves getting *worse* instead of better. It is hard to avoid these value-laden terms. Shedding tears, and showing anger and grief are considered "bad" in our society, yet they are far healthier than locking the pain of grief inside. So the first step to surviving the grief period is to accept that tears, depression, anger, and anguish are all normal, and working through them will help this pain to pass.

There is no recipe for getting through grief. It is your hardest challenge in life. But there are a number of things that have helped others through the ages:

- Pitfalls to be avoided
- Positive steps to take
- Qualities that help: courage, humor, and love

Pitfalls to be Avoided

I have learned to avoid three pitfalls in the grief period: I steer clear where possible of things that rub it in, I avoid playing the victim role when I can, and I try to moderate the swings of the yo-yo effect. Note that in all these I have stressed "if possible." Since the essence of grief is loss of control over something very important to us, a part of the process of learning to live with it is accepting lack of control in that area. A vital part of learning to steer our bark through the shoals of grief is learning that we can manage some things and working to control them without fastening on any particular rule as if our lives depended on it. That is why I have stressed "where possible" in this advice.

To begin with the first, it is just common sense when one is already hurting to avoid unnecessary provocations. When I am faced with doing something during grief that feels like it will be very painful I ask myself, "What will be gained by this?" If the gain is something major for someone who needs me, or some real healing for myself, then I know I can and will do it, for I have never lacked courage. But if there is no major gain for anyone in it, then I have learned not to inflict it on myself, but to spare my energies for the battles that still have to be waged.

Not playing the victim is even trickier, because it is almost the nature of the grief experience to be a victim. Yet we need to rise above the role of the victim as much as possible, and transform ourselves into victors. Think about the people we most admire historically. Most of them were cast in victim situations and rose above them; this is what gave such height to their victories — Socrates, Jesus, Martin Luther King, the many heroes of the Holocaust. Our light never shines so vividly as when we are surrounded by darkness. So while we need to acknowledge our pain and grief, we will never have a better opportunity to let our courage and faith shine through. Forgiveness and real love can never be demonstrated except in the face of wrong and injustice.

Among the thousands of heroes of the spirit who have turned victimization into triumph, Martin Luther King was a shining example. Most major public figures have several speechwriters working on their important utterances. King wrote his own books and speeches, on top of all the challenges of his active volunteer work in organizing and leading civil rights demonstrations and a paying career that was backbreaking in itself. But of all his writings, the one that stands out is his "Letter from a Birmingham Jail." We have read excerpts from it so often in family devotions that my children know much of it by heart.

King had every right to feel victimized. His life and his family's lives were constantly threatened. His words and his actions were under scrutiny from the FBI, the right-wing press, and even middle America, all looking to find fault. He gave up a personal life to stand by his people, and indeed to stand by all of us — for the loss of human rights by any group or any person affects the whole. He landed in jail in Birmingham for leading a peaceful demonstration. He was locked up, isolated from his friends, and subjected to all the humiliations of being a number and a stripped prisoner. Most bitter of all, this devoted minister had just received a sanctimonious letter from well-meaning fellow clergy in his beloved south, criticizing him for his impatient, unwise, and untimely actions. Incredibly, even paper had been taken from him and this entire remarkable letter *was penned on toilet paper!* He sat there and wrote those magnificent words on toilet paper, because these barbs from his fellow clergy wounded him as other criticism could not, yet his response was one of egalitarian dignity, not that of a helpless victim. It is difficult to quote any part of it without quoting all, but a few words may convey adequately that this was no victim writing:

> I am in Birmingham because injustice is here... Just as the Apostle Paul left his little village of Tarsus and carried the gospel of Jesus Christ to practically every hamlet and city of the Greco-Roman world, I too am compelled to carry the gospel of freedom beyond my particular home town...
>
> I cannot sit idly by in Atlanta and not be concerned about what happens in Birmingham. *Injustice anywhere is a threat to justice everywhere.* We are caught in an inescapable network of mutuality, tied in a single garment of destiny. Whatever affects one directly, affects all indirectly . . .

Perhaps you may say to yourself that Martin Luther King was a famous man already and a hero of the spirit, and that you are just an ordinary person over your head in tragedy. I can only assure you that every hero of the spirit was an ordinary person who tuned into God for the strength to do the extraordinary. That strength comes inch by bloody inch, not in some burst of glory. We too can rise to the sublime heights of the spirit of King, but we do it one small step at a time. An important first step is learning not to play the victim in the tragedies that come to us.

So, in ways both large and small, try to avoid playing the victim. Do take time to talk about your grief, but mingle it with constructive, giving activities. Lying down in bed calling friends brings out the victim in me, so I sit up when I want to call a friend, and I intersperse such calls with other activities. Walk with dignity, dress up occasionally, do things that remind you of skills you have and situations where you are in control. It's important to deal with grief openly without wallowing in the victim role, because you can so easily drown in it.

It is important to reject the negative statuses and sometimes the negative names the world assigns to those struck by trauma: we pass from being wife to being widow, from being a CEO to being unemployed, from being able-bodied to being crippled. We need to find positive statuses with which to identify ourselves. My friend Bonnie taught me a lot when she said, "I don't ever think of myself as unemployed in this period. I think of myself as a writer and an organizer, and when I am asked what I am doing I say, 'I am writing a book and organizing a conference.' When this period is over and you and I find new, positive, paid jobs — and we will — one part of me will be glad for both of us. But another part of me will regret the passing of this opportunity because of the wonderful things I have been able to accomplish that I could never do when my time was filled with a paid job." I have passed Bonnie's creative energy and vision on to many more people going through job transitions, for that spirit is contagious, and we all need it. We also need to apply her approach to all other life transitions.

Evaluate the change in your life from this trauma realistically, with the awareness that while much has been lost, many new and old opportunities remain. God has something in store for you beyond the tragedy itself, and you need to remain open to those opportunities when they come. Don't be a victim, be a creative actor, helping to build new forces in yourself and in the world out of experiences that could very well put you down, but won't, because you are a resilient victor.

Finally, temper the yo-yo effect as much as you can. All traumas bring out the manic-depressive in us. Parents of a handicapped child first deny it (up), then accept it (down), then hear of some wonderful doctor (up), then find s/he isn't so wonderful (down), then see the child do something that seemed impossible (up), then see some even worse limitation the next day (down), then hear of some new savior (up)... Avoiding the yo-yo effect, whose emotional ups and downs utterly exhaust you, is hardest of all when you don't know the limits of the trauma. When you are fighting a critical illness, or have a handicapped child whose limits are uncertain, or are facing probable but not certain job loss, you have to struggle with the trauma of the process itself before even dealing with the trauma of the final outcome. The uncertainty and the struggle both sap your energies.

For myself, I have learned to try to let go of the outcome and anticipate the worst, while fighting with a determination that would suggest that I was entirely optimistic about the outcome. This is very hard to maintain, and I do find myself on the yo-yo often, but I have learned to adjust the length of the string. When something good happens, I moderate my hopes about the outcome, and remember that, no matter what, there will be other jolts ahead. When I get a particularly bitter blow, I remember that life holds gifts for me still and that, incredible as it seems, happiness will return some day when the immediate stress passes. The world will never be the same, but we can rebuild positively, taking into account all the hard realities this trauma has brought. We can even use those experiences to rebuild our personal outlook on life, founded on a deeper, more sensitive awareness of the nature of the world we live in.

We can't control our emotions, but we can guide and moderate them. Free will is ours and we can use it to help us cope with our emotions and manage them, while respecting the messages they are giving us. We need to allow our emotions some expression, but must not to be ruled by them. We can consider the consequences — for ourselves and for others — of different ways of expressing our emotions and choose ways that will resolve rather than aggravate our difficulties. Crying with a reliable friend or counselor is good, but dumping our emotions all over our workplace just compounds our problems. Avoiding the yo-yo means managing our lives and respecting our emotions, but not being governed by them.

Positive Steps to Take

Some years ago, a reader wrote in to Ann Landers about how she had dealt with the situation when her adored husband was having an affair with his secretary:

> Sit down with a piece of paper and a pencil. Make four headings at the top of the page. Label the first column "Personal strengths." In it list all the things you have going for you: Education, looks, money, skills, connections, etc.
>
> Head the next column "This helped me before." List all the things that helped lift your spirits when you were troubled: Music, sewing, volunteer work, church, painting, physical exercise, change of scenery.
>
> Head the third column "People I can count on." List your most reliable friends, a favorite relative, a neighbor, a doctor, clergy.
>
> Label the fourth column "New opportunities." List the ways you can get back in the mainstream. Pretend you are a widow. (Emotionally you really are.) Is it a new job you need? A new city? Volunteer work? Back to school?
>
> My salvation was going back to university. I always wanted to get my degree. I not only achieved my goal but found new values. Now I go looking for the person who is sitting alone. I sit down and start talking — or listening. The world is filled with troubled people who need friendship. I learned this when I was in need of help.
>
> The best part of my story is that I kept my husband. Suddenly he was no longer the center of my existence. He began to respect me when I stopped begging for his love, checking on his whereabouts, and making him feel like a heel. Today he sees me as a new person. Just sign me — *reborn*.

All of this is excellent advice, and my only difference with the writer is that I believe the best news is not that she kept her husband, but that she created in herself someone who could be fulfilled whatever he and the rest of the world did. The rebuilding we do during and after trauma has to have that goal. Like that writer, we have to structure our time positively, planning ways of filling it constructively that take into account the changes imposed by the trauma. If you have lost a young child, plan ways of filling some of your time that will be constructive and will fill some of the time his or her care took. If you have lost a limb, plan new activities and develop new skills that you can do minus that limb. One concert pianist who lost an arm made it his mission to search for music he could play with one hand. Take into consideration your gifts, your feelings, your opportunities, and the limits imposed on you by your new situation. Structuring your time a little, not rigidly, gives you something constructive to look forward to when you wake up each morning. Instead of waking just to your aching loss, you wake to something good. This planning also avoids gaping periods of time when your grief can harden into frightening depression. Leave yourself some time to feel and to grieve, but let flexible planning relieve you of the added burden of emptiness that an unexpected traumatic change brings.

One day I got a phone call from a would-be volunteer at the agency where I last worked before retiring. She was exceptionally bright and capable, with several relevant skills to offer. Our first meeting was vibrant for both of us with a sense of God's presence and power. She began to do a special class with our after-school reading club in a low-income apartment building. She also participated in planning our Multicultural Fair, using her outstanding writing skills and media contacts to get us good publicity. Eventually she told me what had brought her to us. She and her boyfriend had broken up, and she knew she needed to find positive outlets to fill this traumatic void. Her experience illustrates the strength of structuring your time: not only did she fill her time, but she used her skills in ways that helped others. Both she and those she helped were better off for her time and talent. She also began filling her life with new meaningful relationships developed through volunteering.

Increasingly common resources are job clubs (a network of people to aid each other's employment searches), parent groups for children with various challenges, and bereaved family groups. All help one another more than any outsider can. One group of ex-employees of a voluntary organization I know meets four times a year for dinner. Some of them were downsized and some quit but all left with a feeling of woundedness that their workplace refused to deal with and their families soon tired of hearing about. They formed their own pastoral care group, knowing that, among themselves at least, the trauma was understood and appreciated.

Historically, time structuring activities have played a part in a lot of creativity, too. Tchaikovsky wrote the whole of his sixth symphony, a work that has thrilled millions with its deep pathos and power, while traveling on a long trip in the throes of a deep depression. Instead of succumbing totally to his depression, he expressed it poignantly in this great music — music that affirms in all who hear it the communality of human suffering and pain, and the way in which creativity can come out of, and bring us out of, that pain.

Qualities That Help

God hath not promised
Skies always blue
Flower-strewn pathways
All our lives through;
God hath not promised
Sun without rain
Joy without sorrow,
Peace without pain.
But God hath promised
Strength for the day
Rest for the labor,
Light for the way,
Grace for the trials,
Help from above,
Unfailing sympathy,
Undying love.

— ANNIE JOHNSON FLINT

There are so many qualities that help us in coping with trauma: empathy, acceptance, reaching out, risking love again, patience, and forgiveness. But in this section I am going to cover just three: courage, humor, and love.

COURAGE

One of the biggest demands on a person in trauma is to find new reservoirs of courage. It takes courage just to wake up in the morning and face a new day. Grace Noll Crowell has expressed it beautifully in these words:

> God make me brave for life; oh, braver than this;
> Let me straighten after pain, as a tree straightens after the rain,
>   shining and lovely again.
> As the blowing grass lifts, let me rise
> From sorrow with quiet eyes, knowing Thy will is wise.
> God make me brave. Life brings such blinding things,
> Help me to keep my sight. Help me to see aright
> That out of dark comes light.

Courage isn't being fearless — it is acting as you know you must when you are scared stiff. The Cowardly Lion in *The Wizard of Oz* was always trembling and scared, but he always marched forward into danger, because he had true courage. Courage is knowing from previous experience just how bad a situation can be, and walking back into it for the sake of some principle. Of course you're afraid — that's just being intelligent. But courage is the will to do what is right in the face of danger and certain pain.

Acting with courage is tough, but it does something for you because it makes you proud of yourself when trauma puts you down and disempowers you. Trauma makes you a victim, but courage makes you a conqueror.

My niece, Laurie, once had the privilege of meeting the white clergyman, William Sloane Coffin, who walked with Martin Luther King through the terrible Chicago march. All the racism and fear of that northern city gathered together and hurled at those civil rights marchers so that it was like walking a gauntlet of hate. The mob lining the streets screamed obscenities and wore the terrible face of hatred. No one knew whether or not it might degenerate rapidly into a race riot, but King and his fellow-leader marched forward calmly, and the newsreels showed nothing but courage in action in all of those marchers. That in itself is a beautiful story: the murky bitterness of hatred confronted by the shining brilliance of loving courage.

But the larger story of courage came from Coffin. "All the time he was marching forward, King was muttering under his breath, 'God, God me *out* of here — this is horrible! I can't take much more of this. Get me out of here...'" Courage is marching forward with the newsreels grinding and the crowd howling, and muttering under your breath, "God get me *out* of here!"

James Russell Lowell, poet of the anti-slavery movement, wrote a famous poem called "Once to Every Man and Nation." One verse in it expresses this faith in the future, shining in the utter darkness of the present:

Though the cause of evil prosper,
Yet 'tis truth alone is strong;
Though her portion be the scaffold,
And upon the throne be wrong;
Yet that scaffold sways the future,
And behind the dim unknown,
Standeth God within the shadow,
Keeping watch above His own.

Courage is walking forward firmly toward that scaffold when you can't see much beyond except the dimness of the unknown. But acting with courage, like most positive actions, is self-reinforcing: each step you take with courage builds your belief in yourself, and in that magical something inside you that many of us call God.

HUMOR

Humor enables one to cope with the impossible by laughing at it. Humor is disarming hell by laughing at the devil. Humor is heady stuff. My first great trauma was being fired from a non-profit organization that I had founded. The board of the agency, not content with firing me once with four months notice, reversed its promise to give me contract terms for the final four months and fired me again, this time with five days notice! When they had thrown me out of my office where they were continuing their meeting *in camera*, I went upstairs and phoned my lawyer: "Guess what, Dianne, I'm trying for a spot in the *Guinness Book of Records*. Who else do you know who's been fired twice in four weeks by the same board from the same job?"

A friend of mine also had a similar experience when her job situation turned ugly while she was actually on maternity leave. She was called in for a disciplinary meeting and brought muffins as a peace offering. When she got home her husband looked at her and said, "There's just something special about you; I don't know anybody else who's ever been disciplined while on maternity leave." What an absurd situation; what could they do but laugh?

More recently, my husband and I were visiting the small hospital Salmon Arm, British Columbia, where we bought our retirement home. We asked the hospital about their range of their services. They asked in turn in what we were especially interested. I spontaneously responded, "My husband has emphysema, and I have cancer, but otherwise we're extremely healthy!" Then we both burst out laughing.

Norman Cousins has written an impressive book about how he defeated what was supposed to be a terminal disease by watching funny films and reading humorous books. Laughter is health giving, and Cousins is only one of the more noted persons who has demonstrated this in one way or another.

Thoreau brought humor to his confrontation with his friend Emerson, when he visited Thoreau in jail. Thoreau had practiced the advice of his own now famous essay on Civil Disobedience by going to jail for refusing to pay taxes for the Mexican War, a war both he and Emerson disapproved of. Emerson looked sorrowfully at his friend and said, "Henry, what are you doing in jail?"

To this Thoreau immediately replied, "Ralph, what are you doing *out* of jail?"

Humor is a part of discharging the anger that threatens to engulf us in the tidal wave of trauma. Humor gives us perspective, but more than that:

humor reasserts our power to handle the situation. It is no wonder that chronically oppressed minority groups have a special style of laughter about the oppressors. They may be able to suspend our rights, but they can't stop us laughing at their absurdities. Humor is healing, it is courageous, and it is powerful.

Love

Loving our enemies is paramount in our response to grief for the sake of our own healing. But you may say, "I just can't feel that way. My particular pain is too much. Or maybe I'm just not enough of a saint. When I'm drowning in grief, I can't feel love toward those who hurt me or let me down."

Of course you can't! Nobody can at her or his moments of deepest pain. Love is not about an emotional feeling — it's about an act of *will*. We can't turn on and off the emotional feeling of love, but we do know what kinds of behavior follow from a loving relationship, and we can systematically follow that path. We can control our *will to love*. Henry Drummond, author of the great classic *The Greatest Thing in the World*, describes loving as an exercise we have to develop by practice:

> The world is not a playground; it is a schoolroom. Life is not a holiday, but an education. And the one eternal lesson for us all is *how better we can love*. What makes a man a good cricketer? Practice. What makes a person a good linguist, a good stenographer? Practice, nothing else.
>
> There is nothing different about religion. We do not get the soul in different ways... If a man does not exercise his soul, he acquires no muscle in his soul, no strength of character, no vigor of moral fiber, nor beauty of spiritual growth. Love is not a thing of enthusiastic emotion. It is a rich strong... expression of the whole round Christian character — the Christ-like nature in its fullest development.

Francis de Sales too describes love as a skill to be gained by practice: "You learn to speak by speaking, to study by studying, to run by running, to work by working. Just so, you learn to love God and man by loving. Begin as a mere apprentice, and the very power of love will lead you on to become a master of the art."

The modern German theologian Jurgen Moltmann, in *The Power of the Powerless*, challenges us:

> Stop asking what your enemy has done to you or to other people. Ask what he *suffers* from, and what the sufferings are which are turning him into your enemy. Ask what God wants to do for him — the God who lets his sun rise upon the evil and the good... Love of the enemy is not a matter for weaklings who are afraid of the enemy. Love is only for the person who has been liberated and who no longer lets himself be impressed by his opponent... Love of one's enemy does not want to conquer him, or convert him to one's own views. This kind of love lives together with the enemy beneath God's sun...

Bernie Siegel, the remarkable American surgeon whose books on healing have sold well for years, describes a significant piece of research in his book, *Love, Medicine, and Miracles*. The researcher analyzed a number of different kinds of smiles, each one of which used a set of muscles. Then he trained subjects to be able to smile in each way on request, and then he asked them to smile the smiles of love and happiness. Even though the smiles were reflecting a request, not a genuine emotion, their immune systems kicked in more strongly as our immune systems do when we radiate love, and they experienced a surge of happier emotions. This was a concrete proof of what I have experienced too, and others have described: when I do loving acts for someone I dislike, my emotions often catch up with my deeds, instead of remaining caught in resentment.

For, surprisingly enough, when we will to love and act on the basis of that determination, our emotions eventually catch up with us. It may take years, but there is a special joy in treating lovingly those that our emotions cannot yet respond to in that way.

Serene I fold my hands and wait,
Nor care for wind, or tide, or sea;
I rave no more 'gainst Time or Fate,
For lo! My own shall come to me.

I stay my haste, I make delays,
For what avails this eager pace?
I stand amid the eternal ways,
And what is mine shall know my face.

Asleep, awake, by night or day,
The friends I seek are seeking me,
No wind can drive my bark astray,
Nor change the tide of destiny.

What matter if I stand alone?
I wait with joy the coming years;
My heart shall reap where it has sown,
And garner up its fruits of tears...

The stars come nightly to the sky,
The tidal wave unto the sea,
Nor time nor space, nor deep, nor high,
Can keep my own away from me.

— "Waiting" by John Burroughs

As "Waiting" reminds us, one of the keys to supporting friends through grief is waiting patiently. The process cannot be rushed, and we have to be there with them through it all. It is crucial that we not tell them to hurry when they need to feel lasting friendship, and we must make time to hear them go over and over it until they are through with it for themselves.

The most important thing a friend can give to someone in grief is real quality listening. This sounds easy, but is much more than cocking a vaguely friendly ear. You need to be able to listen attentively enough in order to summarize the feelings of the other person. This is, for example, a key component of conflict resolution. I remember one particularly good conflict resolution role-play that I was involved in. Afterwards, in the evaluation, one of the key protagonists said that she had felt as if she had been fully heard and understood *for the first time in her whole life!* Eliciting a sensation like that in your grieving friend is your goal. They don't need you to agree with their conclusions, or even all their perceptions — to be heard fully and to be agreed with are not identical. But they do need to feel you truly understand, and that you respect their feelings and see them as normal for someone going through what they are experiencing.

A good listener believes that people will correct their own perceptions toward more healthy accurate ones if allowed to work through them. Good listeners feed back the griever's thoughts to show they understand, and they check that they have caught the most important points. They always validate feelings: anger, pain, grief, fear, joy. Good listeners rarely give advice! People have to come to conclusions for themselves. Even when they ask you for advice, try to get them to think it through for themselves, and you will be surprised how often all they want from you is reassurance that some daring new approach they are considering is acceptable.

Most importantly, good listening is focussed on *helping the griever arrive at a new understanding for themselves.* New understanding need not be a "new idea," all packaged up — it may be simply a shift in meaning, a beginning step toward acceptance, or a different way of looking at some part of the picture. Such new understanding is a real sign of growing and the biggest indication that you are being truly helpful. Don't look for opportunities to tell your experiences, and don't look for thanks; instead, listen for movement in the griever.

Helpful friends are able to accept all the emotions of the griever. They do not squelch guilt, fury, or the most shocking grief. Don't argue with the griever! If they feel responsible for their child's death ask them gently why, and explore that. One of the most revealing exchanges I ever had of this kind was when a schizophrenic friend of mine was describing seemingly absurd fears to me. "Eric," I said, "Why would you think that because you did that, the police would arrest you?" He immediately responded, "That's easy, Ruth — that's because I'm paranoid and paranoids think that way."

Instead of being put down for it or getting into an argument, he was able to laugh at it, and I congratulated him for both his insight and his sense of humor. It was important that I did not voice my spontaneous internal thought, "That's crazy thinking!" I put a question to him, and allowed him to come to his own conclusion, which, in this case, was a creative blend of accepting the confusion inside him and recognizing that it was problematic. In giving him the right to his own conclusions, and respecting them, he was empowered and we were able to laugh together.

The fact is that if it is your friend in trauma, and you are trying to help, one of the greatest gifts you can give is to focus on her or his feelings, and let your own fall into the background. Strangely enough, I find that the ability to do this empowers me, rather than leaving me feeling unheard myself. It gives me pride and joy to be able to play a powerful, supportive listening role. In my thoughts afterwards, sometimes in processing it with a spouse or trusted friend sure to keep the confidentiality, they can give me the hearing of my feelings, if I still need it. But often there is such satisfaction in playing this powerful and spiritually and emotionally vital role of a mature, caring listener that our own emotions are satisfied without being ventilated.

That doesn't mean we accept all negative and destructive *behavior*. There is a difference between accepting emotions and accepting negative behavior. I accept anger as legitimate, but I do not encourage vengeance plots or other detours from the healing process. Suicide, drinking, abuse of dependent people, are all destructive paths we can reject while accepting every feeling the griever shares with us.

Let's try a couple of examples for practice. Suppose a griever says to you: "I keep waking up night after night thinking of her, and seeing the accident, and wishing I had stopped her from going to that wild party. She would have been mad at me, but she would be alive today."

Consider some common, natural responses. "Well, I've often said, kids should not be allowed to drink or drive when they're that young, let alone both together." What's wrong with this one? It's full of the most devastating I-told-you-so blaming of the victim, who is already blaming herself. It reinforces guilt without giving the griever any chance to explore and deal with it.

Another common response is, "Quit thinking about it! It's been three months, and there is nothing you can do to bring her back. It's time you put it behind you. She wouldn't want you to go on like this, and frankly, all your friends are getting weary of hearing you go over and over it." Not quite so destructive, but it still denies the griever the right to deal with her grief in her own time. It guilts her for exploring it, trying to work it through, and tells her she is doing both the dead and the living injury by her natural questions in the grief process. It denies the legitimate right to feel and to explore ones feelings.

A third common response is: "That's ridiculous to blame yourself! You never told her drinking and driving was okay. She made her own choices, and you are not in any way to blame. It's crazy even to think so for a minute." How very well meant that line is, and it may be reassuring to the griever, who wants to hear that the burden of self-accusation is unmerited. But it still does not let her explore her own genuine feeling. Instead, she is told her feelings are unhealthy and crazy. She is denied the right to feel them, and even more, the right to share them.

So what *is* a good response? Remember, the goal is to help the griever make a shift for herself, arrive at a new understanding that is truly hers. So a good listener reflects back, accepting the feeling without acknowledging its validity: "It sounds like you are feeling horribly burdened by feeling responsible for what happened. That's perfectly natural — any caring parent would. We are given an instinct to protect our children, and even when they are full grown it is partly with us. It must be painful to keep going over and over it like that. Why do you feel you are responsible?" There are many shorter ways of accomplishing the same goal: "How awful! I can barely imagine what you are going through. What do you feel you need in order to find some peace over it?"

Another griever may say: "I wish I were the president of the company and could fire him and make him know what it feels like." A common response is, "The whole thing reminds me of the last place I worked. There was this girl who tried to get me in trouble with the boss, and there was another who was on my side..." By this time, the person in deep grief has lost interest. They are not in shape to console you for your past troubles in a somewhat similar mess — they want and need your attention to their current situation.

Another natural response is, "Now, Ben, that stuff doesn't get you anywhere. Revenge will just sour your life." Very true, and very sound advice, but it just aggravates Ben's anger because it seems to him no one cares about his deep wrong. One of the primary needs of victims is for *recognition of their wrong*. A much better response would be "Yeah, after what you went through anybody would be furious. It is so awful to feel helpless, it is natural to want to have the power to reverse things. I'm angry too about what happened to you, and so are all your friends." Such a response frees the griever to say, "Of course I wouldn't really want to hurt anybody — I wouldn't want even that slob to go through what he's put me through. I just wish I could make him understand, so he was really sorry, and so he'd never do it to anybody again."

Such a statement by the griever shows your acknowledgment of his legitimate anger, and your sharing of the burden of it with him has freed him up to move tentatively beyond it, for himself. Don't expect such shifts the first time you give an empowering, listening response that accepts his emotions. People need to go over them a lot, to get the feel and texture of the land, and to share the acres of pain in a normal trauma at their leisure before they are ready to make such shifts. But good listening — accepting all emotions and patiently allowing victims to move at their own speed — facilitates the slow but steady movement of grievers through the dark night of their soul toward new light. This enables them to accept not only this grief, but to be better prepared for other griefs to come.

Try to avoid making heavy demands on those in the grief stage, but do give them the dignity of asking for their help in modest ways that show you still respect and need their skills. Heavy demands can overwhelm those in grief and make them wonder if they will ever have the strength to be useful again, but well considered requests show them that they still have an important place in your life and in the world. If you are not sure of the line between burdening and honoring your friend with such approaches, phrase your request moderately, and accept their judgment as to whether it is a burden or a gift. I was touched when a longtime friend of mine called during a recent trauma of mine to ask my advice on how to deal with a delicate situation in an area of my expertise. I would not have been up to organizing a major conference just then but I was still able to give advice!

Friends entering grief need to hear that there is hope and healing in store for them as well as pain. "I know how much it hurts, and it will go on hurting for a long time. Life will never be exactly the same, but we do come through these things, and when we have learned to deal with them, believe it or not, we gain so much new strength and understanding that in some ways, life is even better." I believe that we need to give grievers both halves of that message, each in the form relevant to them. Grief is not a short process, and they need to know that we accept that it will be long, and that we will be with them. I said to one friend, who was on his way to a particularly brutal firing, "I hope it comes out as you hope, but however it comes out, I want you to know I will be with you all the way through it." And I was, daily, for many months of his deep anguish.

Avoid making promises you can't keep. Enthusiasm and good will can lead you to offer to help in some way that you can't follow through on. This just adds to the sense of desertion for the griever, when false hopes are held out to them. That applies to advice too — don't say "Everyone will forget about this in a couple of weeks," if it isn't so. Don't say, "People will accept your handicapped child just fine," when in fact our society is very mixed in its acceptance of the handicapped. Without false promises, we need to share the hope that there are gifts from trauma, and that our friend can and will share in them.

One person who knows how to be a good and supportive friend is the famous monk Thomas Merton, whose memorable letter to Canadian peace activist Jim Douglass is quoted in the previous chapter. Merton has a lot to say about burnout, discouragement, human relationships, and the hope of working for tangible results. But mingled with all the good advice and wisdom is the one essential in any support letter — plenty of love. We don't have to be as wise or as eloquent as Thomas Merton to have something wonderful to offer. If we give our friends nothing but love, we will have given richly indeed.

CHAPTER 5

Terminated with Extreme Prejudice

Thou lookest thousands of years into the future and then Thou
judgest. What today seems an injustice to man's minute brain
becomes, thousands of years hence, the mother of man's salvation. If what today we term injustice did not exist, perhaps true
justice would never come to mankind.
— Nikos Kazantzakis, *God's Pauper: St. Francis of Assisi*

O
UR FAMILY CHRISTMAS LETTER in 1989 exuded joy over how well
things were going at my job at the Half-Way Society. I spoke of our
large funding increases, our major steps toward empowering clients, my
wonderful board, and many exciting media appearances for myself. We had
even nearly finalized a building project which would provide housing for
the homeless on our site while helping us raise the money to purchase our
building from the Ontario agency which was our "parent." But woven
among these positives were continuing negatives. Staff morale was low, and
I was trying to relieve the overload on them by rushing to fill the new posi-
tions my fundraising had finally enabled us to open. At management meetings we worked hard to find a solution to the concerns expressed by a
number of staff who did not want to work with our most difficult clients.
Men who had been in mental hospitals or had heavy addiction problems as
well as prison records were a big challenge to our badly paid and underqual-
ified staff. In my efforts to solve the continuing caseload and funding
crunches, I had refused even cost of living raises for myself, and had poured

hundreds of extra hours into increasing our funding base by fifty percent in my two and a half years there. Staff representatives participated in our management meetings to brainstorm solutions to these issues. The only solution I rejected was barring the hard to serve from our agency.

January and February were high pressure months for me: staff morale was low, turnover high, pressure for money from our parent agency peaking, and the demands of hiring crushing. I was working a steady 55-hour week, and I did ask my board for more emotional support, but otherwise was enjoying the challenge and was sure we could overcome the difficulties.

In March I agreed to do two speaking engagements in other cities. I got up early on a Friday morning to drive back from these engagements so I could be with staff for an all day training session on how to deal with potentially violent clients. As soon as I walked into the agency, I sensed something wrong.

One of the new managers, Tom, asked to see me urgently. I asked my resource leader and a new staff person to wait for me at the desk, and went into my office with Tom. With a nervous grin, he said, "Don't shoot the messenger, Ruth!" and presented me with an eight-page letter to my board, signed by members of my staff, which had been hand delivered to each of their homes the night before.

Years of familiarity with agency politics of all kinds enabled me, despite my shock, to flip first to the signatures at the end. To my horror I read twenty-five signatures, twelve of whom were current staff in our agency of twenty-six. The others were mostly past staff, each with their own grievances. The letter itself was truly vicious. When examined with care, it was full of contradictions, but devastatingly personal in its attacks on me. It called me incompetent, and accused me of everything imaginable except murder and sexual misconduct. When I thought of my open door policy and the continuing flow of personal kindnesses I had done for staff, I was baffled and shocked. When I considered how hard I had struggled to get them to deal with conflicts with each other openly and fairly, their failure to raise these issues with me appropriately seemed a tragic rejection of all I had stood for.

The next few days began a long nightmare. I had been very close to my board, but this of course imposed enormous strains on all of us. The agency was like two armed camps. Staff members were divided among the signers, those fiercely loyal to me, and those who were straddling both camps, waiting to see where power would fall. The processes the board chose could have been much worse, but they were cruelly unlike the ones I had followed for any staff accused of anything in the agency. After an agonizing week, the board held a meeting that was clearly my trial. They came to a compromise which satisfied no one: they expressed confidence in me, but refused to fire the ringleaders who had spent countless paid hours pressuring people to sign this petition and violating our personnel procedures in every possible way.

Meanwhile, I was due for a long postponed and much needed holiday to visit relatives in England in April. The board decided, on my recommendation, to hire an expert interim administrator in my absence, to do an assessment. They also gave me an extra month's paid holiday to enable her to do a better job and allow a cooling off period for all of us. I left for England with a mixture of relief and anxiety.

Late on the first Monday the phone rang, and my brother-in-law said the call was for me. It was our son, calling with heaviness in his voice. Immediately I feared a catastrophe. "Doug, are you all right?" I asked urgently.

"Sure I'm all right, Mom," he replied hesitantly. I pressed him again, and this time he said, "I'm all right, but it's bad news." All this preparation was making me really anxious. I demanded, "What bad news?"

"It's your job, Mom. It's really bad."

I was so relieved that no one but me was hurt that my overwhelming first reaction was relief. "Oh, if it's only my job, Doug, don't worry about it! Just tell me about it."

It was an amazing story. The provincial branch of our agency had exercised an obscure clause to put our branch into trusteeship, suspended my board, fired me, and gone to the press with their version of reality. I was astounded, but still mainly relieved that I was the primary victim. Remembering that my other work fiasco at the Bail-Out Program had made page three of the major papers, I responded jokingly, "I suppose we made page one of the national *Globe* this time."

Doug replied anxiously to this sally, "That's right — it did!"

The strange thing about the conversation was that my whole focus was on reassuring Doug. I felt so bad that my 22-year-old son was left holding the bag for my work mess, responding to calls from the press, the board, and our friends. I kept reassuring him I was all right, and my first question to my husband after I hung up was, "Do you think I reassured him enough?"

That was shock and parental instinct combined. But Ray realized we wouldn't be doing much sleeping that night. It was so fantastic that we lay there and laughed most of the first hour, a strange laughter born of shock and pain. Nor did we do much holiday-making that holiday. Calls from press and board members gave me bits and pieces of vital information. Things were happening that would affect my whole future, and here I was, far from the action. I thought of going home, but my ticket was unchangeable, and most people told me gloomily that since I could do little, I should relax and "enjoy" my holiday!

Because it was my husband's sabbatical year, he was staying over another two weeks after my scheduled return. We talked about how difficult it would be for me to return alone into that maelstrom. I promised him repeatedly that I would be all right. At the end I added, "Because of my faith, my friends, and because I have learned to handle things like this, I know I will be okay. But *even if* I *am not*, even if it is overwhelming, I will hold together for your sake." I knew it was true, and that living evidence of the love between us warmed my heart.

Coming home to Toronto was worse than anything I could have imagined. Doug and I were the only family there. He was doing exams, and from having been a scholarship student, was suddenly suffering from the effects of his old learning disability. In the midst of everything else he informed me he was probably flunking out instead of graduating! Each day he went to another exam, or stayed up all night hopelessly studying, and reported on his return that the exam had gone terribly. And each day I found out worse things about my situation. My board had tried a legal suit against the provincial association before my return, and it had been rejected.

More sickening to me was the news that my trusted colleagues from the provincial office, on getting their executive's order, had ordered security guards, changed all the locks, and generally made like Latin American putsch artists. Monday morning they had invaded my office, stripped my walls, desk and room of my personal belongings – in the clear view of my staff – and gone around hugging the insurgent staff. The staff loyal to me walked in terror, and rightly so. In the next weeks virtually everyone loyal to me was forced out of the agency. Most incredible of all, the invading provincial staff and the rebel staff had planned and held a victory party, demanding that all my staff attend!

My head swam with visions, like that of Bob, the provincial staff person who had sat in my office peacefully drinking my coffee and discussing the supposedly irresolvable issues six days before my departure, giving me no clue of the intended takeover. Six days later he was stripping the walls of the office where he had so lately been a guest, and was exuberantly hugging the staff who had initiated the petition against me. How could they hate me so much?

Then there was George, the new head of the provincial agency. Despite his obvious sense of rivalry toward me, and despite his having secured power by attacking and persuading the boards to get rid of four other directors (provincial and local), I had offered him my personal warm support when he began that hard job. I had even offered to help write and support a funding grant for his provincial agency, which he had blocked our local agency from applying for. I had recently attended a province-wide brainstorming session in which their board and staff admitted that they had squandered a bequest of several million dollars – due to bad management and overspending – in less than a decade. Yet they were accusing us of "financial mismanagement" when my board and I, mostly in my extra hours, had created a balanced budget and increased our funding base by fifty percent, and even got a special grant to fix up our historic but dilapidated building! How could George hate me so unrelentingly — for it was he who had orchestrated this vicious attack — when I had tried throughout the years to express my support of his good work and of our common values on advocacy issues for the rights of prisoners?

I was buried in grief just from the thought of so much hate and betrayal. The age-old question echoed and re-echoed in my heart: *Why me, God?*

Then I remembered a few other worthy characters who had experienced betrayal and hatred — Jesus Christ, Socrates, Martin Luther King, and all the prophets through the ages. On reflection, I decided I had no special gripes, and was in good company. But the sheer viciousness of the office stripping and victory party, as well as some of the abuse directed at my ex-con staff, overwhelmed me. I called up a friend of mine, whom I had recently supported through a hard time of his own. "Brad, how could they be so vicious? I can deal with the loss of my job, and even with the two-facedness of so many people. But the viciousness of it is just incomprehensible. I can't get a handle on it."

Brad is a wise and spiritual person. His spontaneous answer was strangely comforting to me, then and long after, "It wasn't for nothing that Christ wept over Jerusalem, Ruth." That comment sustained me in many moments when I felt myself nearly drowning in the obscenity all around me. It reminded me that viciousness too is part of human nature. We have to accept it, while working to transform it. I was not uniquely singled out for victimhood; my suffering was part of a long, unceasing parade of people pillaged by man's inhumanity to man.

Letting Go

> Now, all our peace in this life is found in *humbly enduring* suffering, rather than in being free from it. He who knows best how to suffer will enjoy the greater peace, because he is the conqueror of himself, the master of the world, a friend of Christ, and an heir of heaven.
>
> — GERHARD GROOTE, *Imitation of Christ*

The healing process began with a series of steps in letting go. Even before I had left for my holiday, it had begun. The shocking hatred of staff people I felt I had been so kind to bewildered and pained me. I prayed for the gift of forgiveness toward them, I willed what was best for them, and I asked for the grace to *act* in a spirit of forgiveness, whatever I might feel. On the second weekend after that incredible staff petition, God gave me a gift of pure grace. All weekend long I kept visualizing myself on a mountaintop in spring. Snow banks and ice were all around me; streams were half choked with it. But the bright sun was melting and thawing the ice. Clear, pure, beautiful water was running down in gushing rivulets, issuing straight from the mounds of snow and ice. What a freeing, lovely sound! It was a waking dream, and no one had to tell me its meaning. The melting snow and ice were the melting of my anger toward my staff. At first I thought it was a temporary gift, but incredibly, this gift of grace never wholly left me. From that weekend on, I never felt the threat of deep bitterness toward those staff. I felt much more compassion for them, and was able to pray the incredible prayer of Christ, "Father, forgive them, for they know not what they do."

I thanked God for the warming of my heart as that ice cracked, but it didn't solve all my problems. There were new horrors each day. Of the five staff who had organized the original revolt, Lila particularly baffled and hurt me. I had thought that she and I were on the same wavelength. I had done so many things to support her, both personally and professionally. She had never given me the slightest clue of dissatisfaction: yet she had been the most effective of all the complaining staff in alleging that I had forced her to work with men who were threatening to her!

What boggled my mind was an exchange we had had in January. Lila had almost taken another higher paying job. She consulted me openly about it, and I even gave her a reference. I hoped she would stay, but respected her right to choose. She rushed into my office one day, gave me a big hug (such was her terror of me), and exclaimed, "I'm so happy, Ruth — I've decided to stay, because I believe so much in what we are doing and the spirit we are doing it in!" Now I know that *at that very time,* she and the other two leading conspirators were devising that thoroughly vicious petition against me, and twisting arms to get signatures! Replaying over and over her words and actions that day, along with her other actions, was utterly destructive of my peace of mind. So I had to accept that I could not understand Lila. Luckily, our cerebrum doesn't have to be on top of the situation for unconditional love and forgiveness to flow. Love and forgiveness are commitments, not feelings.

The second thing I had to let go of was the job itself. This had been my dream job. I had waited seven months for it from the day I read in the paper of organizational changes that made it a possibility. It had been for me a perfect return to the field of justice that I loved so much, and to which I had given my whole heart and soul. Yet, in spite of this, I found it surprisingly easy to let the job go. Perhaps the sad conduct of the people in the organization made it easier.

Letting go of my righteous anger toward people was comparatively easy. The third and hardest thing I had to let go of was my expectation of decency in the people I had worked with, loved, and trusted. I had to accept their viciousness as part of the human condition. Those words, "It wasn't for nothing that Christ wept over Jerusalem," held the key for me, and they were like pure water on my parched soul. Even Christ had trouble letting go of this one!

Kissing My Lepers

Then Peter came and said to Him, "Lord, how often shall my brother sin against me and I forgive him? Up to seven times?" Jesus said to him, "I do not say to you, up to seven times, but up to seventy times seven."

— MATTHEW 18:2 1-22

One of the books that had been part of my spiritual learning that year was Kazantzakis' *Saint Francis*. In this book, Saint Francis confides in his faithful companion Leo one day, "The one thing I can't abide is lepers." That night God told Francis in a dream that the next day he would meet a leper and embrace him.

This was a bit too much for even Francis. He woke up howling with horror. An almost bitter dialogue followed in which Francis tried unsuccessfully to reason with God. "I gave up Father, Mother, my native village, decent clothes, everything for you. It's not fair — you were listening when I told Brother Leo I couldn't stand lepers, and you picked on the one thing I said I couldn't endure! Isn't all I have done *enough?*" To all this the implacable voice of the spirit of God in Francis thundered back, "Not *enough!*"

That was the end of Francis' brief skirmish with the will of God. From then on, all objections came from Leo. Soon after they began their walk,

Francis heard leper bells. Leo suggested they run, but Francis replied, "If we run away from this, there will be leper bells on every road we choose." When God has a spiritual lesson for us, it keeps coming up till we meet it courageously.

Sure enough, the leper appeared. He was far more loathsome than Francis had imagined. His nose was half gone, his face was a monstrosity, and he stank. Yet Francis ran up to him, kissed him on his excrescent lips, put his own cloak around the leper, and carried him. Finally they neared a leper refuge. Francis moved to uncover the leper, and lo — he had vanished!

Leo was amazed, and thought the leper was Christ come to test them. But Francis was transfigured, for he understood the larger message. Eventually, when he could speak, Francis whispered to Leo, "No, don't you see — it means — it means — that *every time we kiss a leper on the lips, he becomes Jesus Christ!*"

That beautiful story became my challenge, and a vital part of my healing. My husband helped me to see it when I made some reference to my bewilderment about Lila, and he astonished me by saying mildly, "Perhaps Lila is the leper God has given you to kiss." The very force of my revulsion to this thought told me this was indeed my challenge. I tried arguing with my husband, but he didn't even defend the suggestion — after all, it wasn't his idea! I too tried reasoning with God, "Look God, I've been so *nice* about this thing. I have even been nice to George. I've gone so far in forgiving and letting go. I've accepted failure graciously. I've been so nice, if I am any nicer, they may just convince themselves even more that all the nasty things they have done and all their cruelty was all right. You don't want me to condone evil, do you? You can't seriously expect me this year to sing Christmas carols with Lila in the Don Jail if I'm asked to?" All I heard back was that implacable voice, "*Not enough!*" We can be so eloquent about the dangers of condoning evil. Yet all heroic Christians over the ages took that risk, and let God deal with the hearts of their opponents. So I came back to face my challenge with Lila, realizing that she was indeed the leper God was calling me to embrace.

One of the many ironies in this period of my life was that, during the frantically busy period just before the collapse, I had agreed to give a religious talk in Pennsylvania on "transcending traumas." Why I agreed when the topic was different for me and when I was far too busy already, only God can explain. When I would tell people during this crazy period when everything was blowing up in my agency and life that I was going to Pennsylvania to give a talk on transcending traumas, the universal response was laughter. Yet that talk would become part of my healing process and eventually the core of this book. My honest sharing contributed to the healing of many of my listeners. Life is a tapestry of giving, sharing, and receiving, all gloriously intermingled.

One of the poems my opponents had stripped from my walls was ironically titled "Be Gentle:"

> Be gentle with one another...
> The cry comes out of the hurting heart of humanity.
> It comes from the lives of those battered
> With thoughtless words and brutal deeds;
> It comes from the lips of those who speak them,
> And the lives of those who do them.
> Be gentle with one another.
> Who of us can look inside another and know
> What is there of hope and hurt, or promise and pain?
> Who can know from what far places each has come,
> Or to what far places each may hope to go?
> Our lives are like fragile eggs...
> They are brittle.
> They crack and the substance escapes...
> Handle with care!
> Handle with exceeding tender care, for there are human beings
>   there within
> Human beings, vulnerable as we are vulnerable,
> Who feel as we feel,
> Who hurt as we hurt.
> Life is too transient to be cruel with one another.
> It is too short for thoughtlessness.
> Too brief for hurting.

Life is long enough for caring,
It is lasting enough for sharing.
Precious enough for love.
Be gentle with one another.

— Rev. Richard S. Gilbert

Rereading that poem one day, for the first time these words leapt out at me and I fully understood their hidden meaning:

It comes from the lives of those battered
With thoughtless words and brutal deeds,
It *comes from the lips of those who speak them*
And the lives of those who do them.

Suddenly I understood the poem's message: Lila, George and the others were wounded spirits with yearnings as human as my own. They had spoken cruel words and done cruel deeds to me, and the poem was urging *me* to be gentle to them! I saw that they were indeed all my lepers. God had given me the gift this spring of a plenitude of lepers to kiss. Each one that I could truly embrace and kiss with unconditional love would *become* Jesus Christ. This was not a promise of instant conversion in their lives. We cannot control our impact on the lepers of our world. But when we kiss them, we release the Christ force *in us and in the world*. There is no knowing where it will radiate. The one person we are sure to reach is ourselves, releasing in our own hearts the Christ force yearning to break forth, calling us to kiss our lepers. With this burst of understanding, I saw too that when George had taken that poem off of my wall, he had helped to give it to me in my heart, and had given me a deeper understanding of its true meaning.

So I waded through that terrible May and June, struggling to kiss my lepers. I was suspended from my job with pay, and had to adjust to that humiliating role. Accustomed to giving all to my causes, I was being paid to stay away. I gave all I could to supporting my board, which struggled heroically with the appeal process. We also had to work together against the publicity launched against us in an effective first strike campaign. It was a David and Goliath experience. My board had to pay legal costs for their first effort, and I paid and paid — for copying, mailing, and soon, my own legal costs. Everyone urged me to launch a libel suit to try to stop George, whose libel of me was so extensive many doubted I would ever be able to get any job again.

In addition to meetings with my board, I tried to structure my life with constructive activities. I did volunteer work one day a week in the office of Toronto City Councilor Jack Layton. I planned music, walks, and writing, but there were constant new upsets. Both sides were struggling for support from press, and particularly for the loyalty of the funders. Their side had the staff of both agencies to draw on. On our side all the staff time we had was myself, with no secretary, no copy facilities, no office, and under heavy fire.

Finally, in June, the appeal was heard. During those seven heartbreaking hours, I played hymns and waited at nearby Friends House, in case they needed my information, but was not allowed to be present. I knew experientially what "standing your trial" meant. The vile things George and the others had said about me were much of the subject of the day. But at least now I had capable defenders in my loyal board members. Both sides of the story would be presented, whether or not they were truly heard.

Predictably, the provincial board rejected our appeal, backing their own executive and staff. It meant the destruction of the agency we had worked so hard to build. It meant the end of all our dreams for advocacy, community education, and service to those hardest to serve. It meant the triumph of the deliberate lies that had been told. It was heartbreaking, but this too, I had to accept, not as right, but as reality. I had to build anew, somewhere else.

My dismissal letter a week later upset me very little. But around this time my closest friend began to buckle under the strain. She had supported me heroically in the first two months, but had now become almost abusive in her calls, blaming me for getting us into these things. I understood that her anger arose in part from her deep love for me, which gave her pain from my pain. We tried to pull through it, but in the end, we took a recess on the topic. I moved on to a second group of friends, and later a third, because although I moved through the heart of this trauma in just six months, there were few besides my husband who could sustain the amount of time and emotional energy it took during that period. I had to accept the limits in each one's ability to give, thanking them for what they could give, and not resenting what they could not. It was easier said than done, but I understood it and worked on it.

As originally planned, that summer followed a pattern: about three weeks in Toronto, then a weekend or week away at some healing occasion, then another three weeks in town. This gave me a series of breaks to look forward to. But the down side was that return to the city always put fresh salt on my wounds, new bad news, as well as immersion in the old pain. The funding agency, which I had worked for, believed in, and given my all to, in the end accepted the coup as a *fait accompli* and shunned my board and myself. This was one of the bitterest blows. I had to accept that when the funding agency talked about empowerment and inclusiveness, they did not mean they would stand behind agencies whose application of these lofty principles got them bad press. The funding agency, after all, depended on large donations from big business interests, whose acceptance of the most marginalized was very limited. The funding agency understood that all too well.

One of the toughest challenges was waking up in a state of panic, and even experiencing panic in the daytime. I had just enough of a taste of these panic attacks to empathize with those who have experienced them more severely. I learned to breathe deeply, and often to seek some positive activity or outlet. Talking to someone who cared was the best relief, but for that very reason, calling and getting no one when I was already panicky could escalate the panic. I would then have to pull myself away from the phone and force myself into some other activity. Getting out of the house regularly helped. A strange source of comfort was our new, well-running car. Although I was anti-materialistic and not into cars generally, it was the only powerful mechanism in my life that responded to guidance in the ways it was supposed to, and gave a feeling of normalcy and control in my topsy-turvy life.

George and his provincial colleagues never let me back into my office to claim my own belongings. They sent me what they had identified as mine, and beyond that, if I could remember something left behind and name it, I had some chance of getting it back. One of the harshest experiences was coming to my old agency during the preparation for the hearing, accompanied by one courageous board member. We were allowed by the judge managing the process (himself a member of the provincial board) to look in our files for necessary materials for our defense. I was reprimanded if I so much as looked in a non-prescribed direction, and I soon developed a raging headache.

At one point I found a letter from my daughter to me in a program committee file, wherein she had referred to an interesting program in her community that we might develop. I showed the letter to my successor, pointed out it was personal, and asked if I could have it back. She called George, whose response was, "Let her lawyer try to get it for her!" This kind of ruthless vindictiveness was characteristic of George and all of them, but that particular cruelty stuck in my heart longer than most. What had I ever done to merit such pointless and callous abuse? How could the funding agency give money to people behaving in this way and trust them to administer it compassionately for our marginalized clients? I've never seen that letter since, and know I never will in this life.

Sometimes none of this seemed real, for I was still partly in the shock stage, especially from the recent events like the failure of the appeal and the rejection from the funding agency. The grief of the first events mingled with the shock of more recent ones. Some days I said whimsically to my husband, "You know, I really wish it hadn't happened." I decided this peculiarly obvious statement was a way of making it real to myself, and getting in touch with my feelings about its reality.

Another device I resorted to in this early period was a "countdown chart." I marked one hundred days on it, knowing from one earlier trauma that things would gradually ease by that point. Marking the days off helped me through the agonizing early period, even though I believe in living in and appreciating the moment. Seeing the holidays on the chart also helped. Before I was halfway through it, I had abandoned marking it regularly, for my grief work was moving me into later stages and sometimes even toward rebuilding.

My husband's sensitivity in allowing me to talk with him in the middle of the nights was incredible. As for my friends, when I first returned from England, our home answering machine was so full with messages that it sounded like an episode of *This is Your Life*. My favorite was one from Julie Hoffman, with whom I had worked shoulder to shoulder in the field years before. Her warm, booming voice on the answering machine was as familiar as if I had heard it yesterday: "Ruth, this is Julie Hoffman. I just want you to know that you're gorgeous, and I love you, and sometimes you just can't win, but that's all right. Give me a call..." Our mail was graced with beautiful letters, mingled with letters of bad news. One incredible friend used his amazing expertise in organizing political battles to fight against the flagrant injustices I was experiencing; another headed up efforts to start a legal defense fund for me.

With their help and with God's help, I was able to recognize this as a hard transition that offered me the chance to learn grace. I consciously worked at accepting the past realities, and wrenched my face toward the future. I accepted my anger and grief, and talked them out with those I trusted; but I put the brunt of my energies into beginning to build a new future. Yet, I also tried to be patient in accepting that I could not yet know what that future would be. I worked hard at accepting uncertainty and enjoying it, and miraculously, I found I could do it! So, I began to turn my face to the future and accept the fact that while much that had happened was wrong, it had happened, and I had to move beyond it. I could accept the gifts of learning from it without accepting that the wrongs that had happened were in any way justified.

At times I could feel almost grateful to Francine, the provincial staff person who had taken my job, for giving me freedom from the cares of that organization. During the uncertain battle period I did not apply for jobs, for I had still hoped to regain our dreams and right the wrongs that had been done to us. When I did begin to apply for jobs, after the appeal had been lost, I put all I had learned about job search into it. Despite the raw rejection I was going through from my last job, I was able, in large measure, to accept each "no" as a challenge.

For years I had preached to job candidates that landing a job was a matter of timing, job description, and team combination, and not a personal rejection. Now I had a chance to practice accepting what I had said, and I found that I could! I could enjoy the job search, writing the letters, and even more, doing the interviews. Not getting interviews for jobs I felt sure I would fit well in was hardest, but I found I could accept even that with the mildest of grumblings. Each day, I saw this transition more clearly as a return to the infinite opportunities of my twenties, instead of a time of scary uncertainty. I had faith in my ability to handle the job search, and in my ability to overcome the effects of the slander and libel. Increasingly, I took pride in my self-confidence.

Yet it was still a difficult period. Through the lows, I found that God and my friends were helping to pull me through it, and teaching me new lessons from it. More and more of the time I felt normal. One of the gifts of that summer was learning to smell the daisies. As a committed worka-holic, I was poor at relaxing. I learned to accept shorter workdays, fewer engagements, more time for relaxation, walks, and leisure activities. My digestion improved as I learned to accept that quiet, introverted days were a part of God's plan for my life, as well.

But there were moments when I would say to my husband, "I just can't understand how they could have done it. It was so unfair." My heartbreak and grief would surge forth again. The frustrations and uncertainty of the job search sometimes got to me. Expenses incurred during the whole process put me under pressure to get a job, and it was hard not to resent that. We had lent the local agency most of our life savings for the build-ing fund as an interest-free loan. Incredibly, the provincial agency refused to return the funds, and gave us no indication whether or not they ever would. There were so many hard things to bear, but I remembered, like Etty Hillesum, that when I showed myself ready to bear them, the hard was directly transformed into the beautiful. It was so often so that toward the end of that strange summer, I caught myself saying, "It's been a won-derful summer." I was referring to being able to share it with our adult children, who were with us, but it was also true for the growing I was experiencing.

In late August I was booked to represent Canadian Quakers at the Eighth UN Congress on Crime and Prevention in Cuba. Cuba was an oasis, where my peers in the field treated me with dignity. I made new contacts there that opened doors for service beyond Canada. I returned to a series of job interviews, ending with the interview for my last job before retirement. I concluded that interview with these words: "Many people seek security in locks, doors, and neighborhood suburban ghettoes. I have found incredible strength in the loyalty of my friends, my family, and my faith. My security is my ability, with those supports, to endure with grace whatever comes to me in the future. What greater security can there be?"

That kind of security is available to each one of us. When we learn to accept it, we will have less need to attack one another out of our own fears. Victor Frankl, who developed his theory of logotherapy from the pain of his experiences in a concentration camp, has summed it up in *Man's Search for Meaning*:

> If you are confronted with a fate you no longer can change, say an incurable disease, you may find the highest conceivable meaning. Then you have the opportunity to bear witness to human potential at its best, which is to turn tragedy into a personal triumph. *To turn your predicament into an achievement is to reach the peak of your capabilities as a human.*

CHAPTER 6

Acceptance

One day my wife said she thought the darkness could be part of God's training for the job. I came to accept that view. Fear itself can be *used* by God to equip us for our tasks, so long as we take the right attitude to it and do not let it cow us into surrender... Like all men, I love and prefer the sunny uplands of experience, when health, happiness and success abound, but I have learned far more about God, life, and myself in the darkness of fear and failure than I have ever learned in the sunshine. There are such things as the treasures of darkness. The darkness, thank God, passes. But *what one learns in the darkness, one possesses forever.*

— LESLIE WEATHERHEAD, *Prescription for Anxiety*

BEFORE WE CAN GAIN THOSE gifts of the darkness there are hours of what seem like endless pain stretching before us. In the early days of grief we learn what our most vulnerable times and sore spots are. Once you have learned yours, accept that you will then be especially vulnerable for a long time to come. However, there will be better times.

Accepting the Cycle

In living through my deepest traumas, I have learned that nights, especially nights alone when my husband was away, were the hardest. Early mornings were equally tough: I alone was awake, trying to occupy myself quietly with a sleeping family all around while I felt tired and depressed from my poor night's sleep. As the family got up and the day's routine took over, the day usually got better.

That was my cycle, and once I got a handle on it, I quit waking up in a panic. I began planning different ways to occupy my toughest hours, and knew that part of my growing was learning how to slog through them. So we must learn our particular cycles, find ways of coping with the hardest hours or days, and accept that while they will still be hard, we can get through them. That acceptance lightens the load and takes away the panic.

In the midst of one trauma I kept waking up around three a.m. Talking with people about this, I found to my surprise that many of my friends would wake at that hour and fret about their problems. The French call this *les nuits blanches*. We decided to form a prayer club, the three a.m. club, and when we woke at that hour, instead of stewing about lost sleep and about issues we could not solve at that hour, we would say to ourselves, "Oh good — I'm in the prayer club tonight! " We would bend our energies to praying for each of the others. It was no magic solution, but it took our cycle and turned it into an offering to God and to each other. It also recognized the solidarity of common suffering and mutual support.

Accepting the Series of Continuing Hurts

Trauma would be easier to cope with if it came in one great shock, and then no more. But every trauma comes as a series of blows. Just as we begin to cope with one, another comes along. A family begins to accept a serious injury to their child, and then is told the school can't accept the child in her new condition. They struggle through that one, and then a relative makes an utterly tactless remark — and so it goes, on and on. Just as they begin to feel they can cope with the blow, some new event — often based on the failure of others to support them sensitively — knocks them down.

The key again is acceptance. You're not weak when new blows knock you down again. Each new blow carries its own shock, grief, and rebuilding, and it's tough getting new shocks while you're still struggling through the original grief. Accept that any major trauma carries a series of blows with it; you coped with the first news, and with each new wave you crest, you become stronger. As Nietzsche said, "That which does not kill me makes me stronger." Bernie Siegel refers to pain and suffering as God's reset buttons, comparable to the button on a dishwasher or a computer that gives the apparatus a chance to overcome some obstacle and try again. There will be other hurts, but every one you weather makes the next just a little easier, for you are learning the hardest lessons life offers.

There is a story about an old sharecropper in southern United States who resolved to praise God in all things. His foot developed a blister and he said "Praise God!" Then his best hoe broke, and somewhat more reluctantly he said, "Praise God!" He found weevils in his flour, it poured down rain just when he needed to reap, and he kept praising God. Finally he went indoors to shelter from the weather, looked up and saw a leak in his roof, and then the roof began caving in. At this point he looked up to heaven, shook his fist at God and shook his head and exploded, "Lawd, this is gettin' plumb ridikerlous!" We often feel like that man, and again, humor helps us cope with the series of continuing hurts that come with most major traumas. But patience, courage, and love all have their parts to play.

Etty Hillesum, whose last year of life in concentration camp was one continuous immersion in trauma, wrote, "Oh God, times are too hard for frail people like myself. I know a new and kinder day will come. I would so much like to live on, if only to express all the love I carry within me. There is only one way of preparing the new age, by loving it now within our hearts. Somewhere in me, I feel so light, without the least bitterness, and so full of strength and love. I would so like to help prepare the new age." Miraculously, through her writings which reached the world through the persistence of a friend, Etty Hillesum continues to help us prepare the new age, and to witness to the fact that we *can* accept the cycle of continuing hurts.

But even without fresh hurts, grief comes in waves of ups and downs, and we need to accept the normality of those too. With the passage of the seasons, our children grow; and, with the passage of the waves of grief pains, we too do our growing.

Accepting Uncertainty and Transition

One of the hardest things to accept in life is uncertainty. It is easier to accept almost any horror than to live with uncertainty. The yo-yo effect becomes violently destructive, and we oscillate between radiant hope and utter despair. This is the reason why the families of the disappeared can only find peace when a body is returned. The yo-yo of hope, that their loved one is still alive versus the anxiety that they are still suffering, is a greater burden than grief itself.

Some years ago, I was in the doldrums of job-hunting after a traumatic job loss. I'd been through three months of searching, and things were not coming together. I went to one job interview where it seemed I had a good chance. They became very interested in my bad experiences on the last job, and found them entertaining. They thought the behavior of my opponents was absurd, but they were still exploiting my suffering for their entertainment. I found out afterwards that they had picked their candidate before my interview, and that the whole performance was a farce! I was so humiliated; I sobbed my heart out. I lay there, feeling I had hit a new low.

Then it came to me that the lesson God had for me in this experience was *to learn to live with uncertainty.* I had to accept the possibility that I might never have a meaningful job again, and that I could have a good life in that situation. I had to accept that I could learn to be *creatively unemployed.* As soon as I got that message, I was transformed from self-pity to a sense of profound empowerment. That experience has helped me since then with many other large and small trials with uncertainty. Each time I identify this as another situation of uncertainty, I remember again, "I *can live with this uncertainty the rest of my life."*

I know now that I can accept any transition for what it is and glory in the power of having conquered the dragon of uncertainty. Instead of wishing all the time for it to be over, resenting the things that caused it, I welcome each moment of uncertainty as a golden opportunity to learn better how to cope with it, and I know that I can do so forever, if that is to be my future. If I find myself slipping back into the feeling of flailing around desperately in the ocean of uncertainty, I remind myself of that experience. I stop struggling, relax and begin to float, for I know this is a training opportunity for one of life's big challenges, one I have met before and can, with God's help, meet again.

Uncertainty and transition are closely linked. Not long ago I read an excellent book on coping with transitions. It made the point that all transitions — even positive ones like marriage, parenthood, and promotions — are stressful, and all have three phases. The first phase is saying goodbye to the old, and yearning for what we are leaving behind. The second is in some ways the hardest: in it we have left our safe harbor, but the new shore is not yet in sight. This is the limbo stage of transition, hardest for most people because it is full of uncertainty. There is no clarity on where we are going or why. The third stage is beginning the new, and it is in many ways the easiest, but it still carries with it the stress of learning hard new roles, and the fear of failing at them. We wonder if we have chosen correctly, and echoes of the grief for our lost safe harbor trouble us from time to time.

This seemingly obvious observation, that all transitions have a beginning, a middle, and an end — a farewell, search, and discovery — has given me profound insights. The same book advised me to write out the major transitions of my life, and how I had coped with each. I learned that my pattern, like that of so many, was to cling yearningly to the past, in spite of being a radical about change in many ways. That discovery has enabled me to identify transitions and consciously turn my face to the future during them.

Instead of fearing the limbo stage, and longing for it to be over, I have discovered in it the joy of a return to the infinite potential of adolescence, when the whole world of choices lies before us, and our selections have not yet narrowed our options. There is excitement, energy, and wonder in the uncertainty of transition! All we need do is welcome it, glory in it, seize it as an opportunity instead of pining for the stability of established roles that lie behind us, which will come again in the future.

These three stages of transition correspond closely to the four phases of dealing with trauma. Shock is saying goodbye to the old; it is the hard wrenching of partings and farewells; and because it is usually not chosen by us, it is doubly hard to accept. Grief is the limbo stage: we know the past is gone, but we cannot yet see the shore of a new life without the thing trauma has taken from us. Grief, like the limbo state, is usually the longest and hardest stage. Finally, acceptance, healing, forgiveness, and reintegration are parts of building the new life. The pain of our trauma will never wholly leave us, but we have integrated it into the new life to which this transition has brought us.

Even the greatest of tragedies can offer us opportunities that can be positive, little as we would have willingly chosen the whole new direction and all that brought it about. I saw a video about an American woman whose husband was shot to death and whose only son was severely wounded by a completely demented man who had had no difficulty getting a gun in his clearly paranoid state, and who opened fire on a crowded New York commuter train. The widow fought hard for her son's life, but she also fought hard for reasonable gun laws, which are exceedingly lax thanks to the self-centered and powerful U.S. gun lobby. There is overwhelming evidence that inflated homicide rates in the U.S. are largely due to the arsenals that lies in the homes of many of its citizens. Statistically, evidence shows that those guns are more likely to be turned on spouses, children, and family members, accidentally or intentionally, than they are against intruders. Despite all this they go on screaming for the right to bear arms.

The widow was opposed by that gun lobby, and her Congressman was no help at all. In desperation one day she said to an interested press, "I could do better than that man is doing!" The press picked it up as a headline that she was running for Congress, not her intention at all, but her friends eagerly urged her to do it. She ran, was elected, and played a key part in working for better gun laws. She played entirely new, major roles in many areas, roles she never would have chosen voluntarily, due to events which she would still have undone if life permitted. But it didn't, so she learned to turn her face forward, to prevent similar tragedies for others, and in doing so, used her life and her abilities to build a better world, and, in the process, discovered new talents and capacities in herself that she had not suspected were there.

So trauma is just a particularly stressful kind of transition. In accepting uncertainty, we sail courageously through its most troubled waters. Limbo is a hard state to endure, but the infinite potential of uncertainty is something we can try to welcome.

How can we find "infinite potential" in something as agonizing as the loss of a child or a spouse or a limb? By looking at all the new directions that loss leaves us – directions we would not have chosen – we can move forward with creative strength. Helen Keller would probably have been an insignificant southern belle had scarlet fever not robbed her of sight and hearing. Frank Laubach would have spent his life presiding over small university politics had religious bias not deprived him of a college presidency and sent him on paths that led him to become a pioneer in world literacy. I would not be writing this book, nor have learned the biggest truths in it had I not twice been abused, betrayed, and cast adrift in work situations where I know I deserved far better. You too can find the grace to see a rainbow of opportunities through the dark skies of your transitional uncertainties.

Accepting the Gifts

One of the deepest challenges to my faith was seeing my beloved mother deteriorate for ten long years from Alzheimer's disease. How could a just and loving, all-powerful God allow one of the most beautiful spirits I have ever known to lose not just her intellect but even much of her incredible tranquil patience and radiance of spirit, so that the essence of her spirit seemed mocked by this disease? I never found an intellectual answer to this question, but eventually I gained spiritual acceptance that God knew what S/He was doing, and I didn't have to.

We cared for Mom in our home during much of this period, and it seemed an appropriate witness to all she had taught me about love. Yet, I was troubled. I worried that my children would remember not the spiritual giant I had known, but the dreadful disease that inhabited her body. But in the years after her passing, each of them has let me know in their own special way that they had seen her true spirit shining through. The following excerpt of an essay called "Journey's End," which my elder daughter Corinne wrote, expresses what the gifts of this suffering with my mother were for her:

. . . My favorite journey during my childhood [was] the trip to Grandmother's house. It was Grandfather's house also, to be sure, but I preferred G-Ma. Grandfather had a jar of peppermints, but I never liked mints. I liked Grandfather, but he sometimes got mad if we played too boisterously. I should pay tribute to him, however, because it was he who wrote the only poem that was ever written to me. It was a sweet little piece to an 8-month-old baby, and though it was not immortal poetry, it's more than the child of many a famous poet got. But G-Ma used to play with us, and adored us, and we adored her — those days.

I have to say those days because there came a time when I didn't adore my Grandmother at all. The last years of her journey were very difficult, because she lost her memory gradually, on her way. She kept her warm heart and conscience, her faith and her healthy constitution, almost to journey's end, but lost her memory little by little.

There was a period between my early love and before I utterly sympathized with her when I neither liked her nor respected her. Even if you loved her very dearly, it was impossible to live with her without frequent angry arguments. Perhaps if we had agreed with her confused ideas, life would have been more comfortable, but I don't believe that. Even when she believed us, we had to repeat the basic facts of her life to her over and over endlessly every night for an hour or more. Later on, she would come to us kids as soon as we came through the door after school, and start asking questions to us.

Things did not improve with her. Why then did I return to loving her? I grew older and wiser, yes, but at base there is no reason for love. I discovered pleasure in entertaining her, in playing with the flood of questions, like a child playing with the flow of some little stream, directing it here and there by putting stones in its path, and digging a new path for it.

It was fun to ask her about the old days. She could remember a lot that happened a long time ago, although she could not remember what had happened that day — and hearing her play the piano, because she was very good at playing the piano after losing every other talent. Every time she would want to help Mom as much as she could, and towards the end, she was cute the way little children are. When a Jehovah's Witness came to our house and tried to persuade her to buy a copy of a pamphlet for twenty cents, she answered, "*Twenty cents?* Do you think we keep *that* kind of money in the house?"

But she went very quiet in the end. She was in hospital for the last months, and we used to bring songs to sing for her, because she couldn't talk much, or understand books. She would watch or sing along or cry. She did not rage against God or life anymore, but it's hard to say whether she was at peace, until the end of her journey came at last, and the great healing.

I don't know how the end of my journey will be. I can't but hope it will be smoother than the end of G-Ma's journey. But if I have to feel the same anguish, I hope I will be lovable under the pain as she was, and I hope I will be able to run to the end of my journey singing, though crying.

What greater gift could life have brought us than to enable our child to see the beauty in her grandmother through all that anguish, and to prepare Corinne herself to end her life's journey singing, though crying. Chapter 10 of this book talks in more depth about the gifts trauma can bring.

Accepting Others as They Are

Peace to you, my friend
For as I know not your aspirations
In your darkest hours
I know you are beautiful
As you are
As you wish to be,
For God is upon your every hour.
No burden should you carry
For the sparkle in your eye
Is the spirit that is simply you.
Peace to you, my friend.

— N.R.

The young man who wrote those beautiful lines lived in a dark world of schizophrenia much of the time. Despite the profound understanding that these lines show, he escaped from his darkness into suicide before he was thirty. Loneliness is all around us, and we can only escape our own by reaching out with sensitivity and touching the loneliness of others.

There are two groups of people we have to be especially careful with during our grief: those who have hurt us and our friends.

Loving the Opposition

If your trauma involves opponents who, by their actions or inactions, have hurt you, you face some special problems. How do you fight on the issues while loving the opposition? How do you love the opposition, without repressing the legitimate anger you have to get out and work through?

One help is the anger of friends. I find it very healing when persons much farther from the center of my storm express themselves very strongly about the obscenity of what is happening. Their anger acknowledges the wrong for me. One of the basic needs of victims is that society *acknowledges the wrong done to them*. It affirms your sense of reality. You know you're not crazy to feel those waves of hurt and anger. Friends can get some of your anger and pain out for you by raging on your behalf. Righteous indignation is a very healing gift from friends and bystanders. In a recent crisis I faced, I got a beautiful message from a friend who wrote, "I looked all over for a suitable card for you, but I just couldn't find one that said *damn* in big enough letters." His open anger put me in touch with anger I had repressed, and gave me permission too to be angry.

Beyond this, the secret of loving an opponent is loving them because *you* deserve it, not because *they* do. Love doesn't mean liking all the rotten things they have done. I feel compassion for their lack of understanding of the deeper values of life. After all, I only have to live with the direct impact of their selfishness and hatred a few hours a day and a few years at worst — they have to endure themselves twenty-four hours a day all their lives!

Moreover, I remember that my friend Hanne said so eloquently, "God's time is not our time." Sooner or later truth will out, and behavior that runs counter to the life forces of the universe will run into problems. I don't need revenge, but even if I did, their own selfishness will prevent their living long at peace in a world which requires us to share. Yet, whether I ever see any justice or not, the only person I can truly influence for sure is myself. If I grow more loving from this experience, then I am a big winner, no matter what the world around perceives.

Over the years, I have learned three basic lessons in risk-taking love, whether applied to the world's rejects or to the world's powerful but pathetically immoral leaders. The first lesson is that the object of your love risk is unlikely to respond in the way you would like. One brave experiment in loving is not likely to overcome a lifetime of deprivation and rejection for my street and prison friends, nor is it likely to overcome a lifetime of power abuse in the corporate world. So invest in these risks, but don't expect that your greatest reward will come from the object of your affections. The second lesson is fairly obvious: the only person you are sure to change significantly is yourself. For when we expand our ability to love, we are transformed, whatever the recipient does or feels. But the third lesson is the surprise. Whenever I have engaged in risk-taking love, there are bystanders who are influenced by it, often people I never knew or never expected to know of my adventure.

I once received a letter from Australia from someone who had gotten hold of my pamphlet *The Risk of Loving*. He had been deeply moved by the journey I described, in which the first prisoner we had loved, bailed out, taken into our home and advocated for, had proceeded to leave us, and a number of other generous Quakers, with co-signed loans for which we were liable. This Australian stranger had also engaged in the risks of loving, and my pamphlet had inspired him, as the experience did for me, to learn something about who to co-sign loans for, but never to abandon risking love for anyone who seemed ready for it.

Closer to home, I have never engaged in risk-taking love without having people nearby, known or unknown, tell me how much my experience and venture have meant to them. The people who catch the spirit are those already ripe for it, but for each of them, it is a next step forward, a strong call to expand their own ventures in love. So, in daring to love those who have offended and hurt us, we may not reach their hearts — for only God can do that – but we will reach our own hearts, and liberate ourselves from the fatal pull of bitterness and hatred. We will also, amazingly, just when we feel most vulnerable and useless, inspire others in ways we could never predict. So if I grow more loving from this experience, then I am a big winner, no matter what bystanders are able to perceive.

One does need to fight for justice on specific issues, but one should hate the sin and love the sinner. The wisdom to know when a cause is lost, and how to accept that loss, is one of the most elusive. The world is too quick to shrug its shoulders at injustice, and tell victims to swallow it. Sometimes it is right to go on demanding justice, but sometimes the odds against it are so great that it is better to turn our backs and move on. I will never say such situations are just, or allow wrong to be called right, but while firmly labeling them for the unholy wrongs they are, there comes a time when I must move on, for the rest of the world is unwilling to face them. This is particularly true when the wrong is to myself.

One incredible family had their seven-year-old son killed by a reckless teenage driver. Instead of taking the road of bitterness, this family visited the teen, trying to understand the tragedy that had taken their beloved child. They found the older youngster lacking family supports and desperately hungry for something more. The family made the amazing decision to take their son's killer in to live with him, and assist him in furthering his education. They went to court with him to urge leniency, and they took him into their hearts.

People who are told this story sometimes feel it was disloyal of the family toward their own son; others think it was kind of a prolonged revenge, by continuously exposing the older boy to the pain and loss of the family he had bereaved. In fact, the proof of the act's motive was in the long-term impact on the boy and the bereaved family, which was tremendously good to both. But not every observer was large enough in spirit to be able to grasp the magnificent vision and heart's call that made such a miracle to possible.

So, while one can question the motivation of the giver, or the effect on the recipient, I don't believe we can control either one. Harold Loukes said eloquently, "An act of love that fails is just as much a part of the divine process as an act of love that succeeds, for love is measured by its own fullness, not by its reception." If the receiver of understanding love experiences guilt, perhaps she or he can grow even from that guilt. For guilt, when it is not destructive, incapacitating self-blame, can be the foundation for healthy change. But the greater hope is that the receiver can catch on to the example, and learn to practice the unconditional love he has received. The story of Les Miserables is of the criminal Jean Valjean learning to practice living the unconditional love he has received from the bishop.

But can the giver give such love without feeling guilt themselves? Guilt toward others who were wronged, or guilt for treating this sinner as kindly as others who have not sinned? I can only say that this incredible art of separating the deed from the doer is a mystery to me, too. I do believe we have to recognize the wrong in some fashion, and then go on from that point.

Personally, I have achieved this gift of grace in three ways: by an act of divine grace, by positively confronting the issue, and by letting it die of old age. Sometimes God simply gives me the grace to love, I know not why.

The third method, loving by letting an old grievance starve to death, I learned from a Quaker friend of mine who offended me deeply in our Meeting for Business one day. She treated me in a way that most people would describe as unforgivable, and I knew it would be difficult to feel close to her ever again. But our relationship never had been very close, so I went on being civil to her, and gradually put it on the back burner. Some years later she rushed up to me after a Meeting one day, telling me how much she admired me and that I was the conscience of the Meeting. To my surprise, I realized that I had completely forgotten, in any feeling sense, my old grievance, and that our relationship had healed simply by starving the grievance to death and letting it go.

Lowering Expectations of Friends

A friend of mine urged me to move on from a particular wrong I had experienced with the following words: "We have to let it go, not because it is right, but because people can't deal with it, and it will minimize further harm to us." She was a good and supportive friend, but she was right, of course, and her words point to the next challenge: we need to lower our expectations of friends. This book is full of what I believe are sound recommendations for friends supporting those in trauma. The reality is, however, that most people don't do these things. I have come to accept that this is not because they are bad or disloyal, but because our society doesn't train us in the understanding of trauma.

So it is no use beating your head against a stone wall, getting bitter about every friend that has failed to come through for you. It's also true that your own crisis is so large you can lose perspective on the need that others have to keep their lives going. One needy friend of mine said after his suicide attempt: "If I have so many friends who care about me, how come none of you were there when I phoned you that night?" If this seems very immature to you, ask yourself if you have never felt irrationally deserted when you called someone about some urgent need and they were out.

Of course it hurts when you know that a little more effort from a few people who say they care could help you turn your issue around. But you need to accept that each one gives what they feel they can. Everyone has a different sticking point. You need to begin refitting yourself into the world by accepting people's priorities. Up to a point, you do need to educate people on your needs, and on justice issues. Beyond that hard-to-define point, spare yourself deeper grief by raving no more against fate and the limits of the world around you.

It may help too to consider some of the reasons why friends let us down. The literature on victims of crime has been very useful in learning more about victims of trauma generally, and what their healthy needs are. What that literature indicates is that revenge is not a primary need, but a secondary reaction when we fail to meet the five primary needs of victims, which are:

- Answers
- Recognition of wrong
- Safety
- Restitution
- Significance — a larger meaning to the suffering

Because many of these needs are not consciously recognized in our society, most people are groping to find or give them, either as victims or friends. As a result, they are rarely met even to a minimal level. You need to recognize those needs in yourself in relation to your trauma, think out how they could be met, and reach out for them. But most friends are still at least partly denying your need because of one or both of the two great myths: trauma is exceptional, and it is short. So recognize that most of your friends will not understand these needs in you, and will not satisfy many of them for you. Socially and spiritually, we are in our infancy in learning to heal trauma in each other. That doesn't mean you shouldn't try to deepen your own empathy and ability to respond to others through this experience.

By lowering our expectations of friends, we keep each friend for the special qualities they have. That is part of unconditional love. As a friend's grandfather was known to say, "You have to love people for their good points." Some friends are fair-weather friends, not because they are cowards or disloyal, but because they just don't know how to cope with trauma. If you want to, you can keep them through your trauma, while gently teaching them a few things about it. Others are foul-weather friends who are a tower of strength in your trauma, but who don't know as well how to rejoice with you when good times come again. Cherish them for what they are, and find ways to include them gently in your joys as well. A few are all-weather friends, and these are ones you will become especially close to when you've been through changeable weather.

Some people really do turn their backs on you in time of trouble, and these you need to let go. But you need to distinguish between healthy winnowing, which trouble causes, and writing off the inadvertently inept. Trauma challenges us to accept lovingly the many colors of friendship, and to nurture our friends' growth through it, as well as our own. We can only do this if we lower the expectations that have been raised by the heightened need of our situation. Lean on the few who truly understand, but accept the rest as people who may well have an important place in some future chapter in your life.

It is tempting to rely entirely on one or two superb friends whose understanding surpasses that of all the rest. Indeed, it would be foolish not to deepen our relationship with friends like these and spend more time with them if they are available. But friends with such gifts generally have busy lives of their own and others they are helping. Even if they are willing to give you priority for the months and months of your journey through the tunnel of grief, sometimes illness, trips away, or other events will make them less available to you. Then if you have relied wholly on them, you feel abandoned and you really are in the basket! Moreover, even the most empathetic and giving friends will be glad you share with several, and can share with them too the wisdom and strength and new growth you gain from visits and talks with others. So make sure your outreach to the friends you count on most includes at least three to six different people.

There are many colors to friendship; old, new, close, casual, fraught with conflict, smooth, spiritually deep, superficial, daily, once a year... All friendships are precious and should be treated as among God's greatest gifts to us. Fair-weather friends and foul-weather friends both have their places in our lives. Some friends depend on me more, some friends I lean on more; the relationships I find most satisfying are most mutual, but all have a place, and all are part of God's precious gifts to me for this lifetime. John Wesley wrote to his nephew, whose choice of the Catholic faith was a challenge to both famous Wesley brothers, "Though we cannot think alike, may we not love alike? May we not be of one heart, though we are not of one opinion?"

For all the advice in this section of many ways of lowering our expectations of existing friends, there is another gift to be gained in this time of darkness. God guides us to those who can and will help us out profoundly. They may be acquaintances, slight friends, well-known friends, or brand new friends who turn up just when we need them most. What distinguishes them is their ability, even their zest, for walking this journey graciously, warmly, triumphantly with us. They are God's special gifts to us for this trauma, and it may seem easy and obvious to welcome them with glad hearts. But if we are too preoccupied with how existing friends have let us down, we can fail to welcome the new.

An excellent book, on the gifts of an unhappy childhood, points out that we need to stop expecting deficient parents to give us as adults the love they failed to give us as children; we cannot force them to change.

Instead, while encouraging healing in that relationship however far it is possible, we need to welcome the love that surrounds us from new people in our many adult years. By letting go of old friends unable to give what we need in trauma, we make room to welcome those special gifts from God: new friends who come to us out of the darkness, God's gifts to us precisely for this period.

CHAPTER 7

Cancer: The Great Leveler

You have to walk forward through the walls of fire and water
  To the music of the magic flute
Closing your eyes to the barriers,
  And trusting that whether you survive or not
The magic of the music will survive
  And you will gain by your effort.

— RUTH'S DIARY, 2000

THIS VISION OF WALKING WITH divine music through life was inspired by our favorite video, a brilliant Ingmar Bergman film of Mozart's truly magic opera, *The Magic Flute*. The final scene shows the hero and heroine doing what these words portray. By closing their eyes and tuning into the magic flute they are playing, they are able to keep walking forward through the horrors of fire, water, and death, in its many faces. One of the things they discover is that when you do this, some of the barriers prove to be illusory — but the pain and terror of others remain real. The secret is that being tuned in to the heavenly music helps you to carry on through them. I must have seen the video three times before the full import of that scene to today's world penetrated to my soul, but once I got it, it became an ongoing vision of inspiration and courage. More and more, I have learned to tune myself in to the divine music, step forward slowly but steadily, and find so many barriers melting, and others still resisting painfully, but possible to cross.

You've Got Cancer

In May 1999 a barrier we had not expected, which few of us ever expect, suddenly thrust itself into our path. While I continued to feel my high energy, bouncy self, a lot of blood appeared in my urine. I dutifully went to the doctor, who sent me to a specialist, who did various tests. Within days, I found myself on a table, having survived an embarrassing and uncomfortable exploration of my urinary tract. But the reactions of the various technologists taking pictures earlier, and the fact that I was scheduled last of all his patients that day led me to expect something. I reasoned three possibilities: just a minor problem, no tumor; a tumor, but not malignant; or a malignant tumor. My customary optimism was modified enough so that I was anticipating the middle outcome: a tumor that was not malignant.

However, the surgeon called me over and showed me the pictures of my kidney. He explained to me that he would do tests, but that there were two tumors, and from the nature of the tumors and their location, he was virtually certain they were malignant. The good news was that they were contained, and he was hopeful that with removal of my left kidney, where they were, the cancer could be completely eliminated. I asked: "What if the biopsy shows no malignancy," and he said, "Then I would do a further test."

"You're that sure they are malignant?" I asked, surprised.

"Yes," he said quietly, apologetically, with traces of tears in his eyes.

He asked if I had any other questions, and if I was all right. His nurse said she would accompany me to the desk. They were so gentle and supportive, and I was still in shock, and partly focused on gratitude that I had gotten through the examination with as little pain and embarrassment as I did. As so often when we are in shock, I wanted to ease the mind of the bearer of bad news, and I thanked the doctor for the way he had handled it.

His next words were typical of this wonderful doctor's sensitivity. "You're not supposed to thank me for news like this!" he protested. But because of the way he had handled it, I did feel gratitude, and I was glad I had expressed it. Besides, because of my fundamental optimism I was convinced this was a minor brush with a big terror, and that, as the doctor said, the operation would take care of it all. I knew I would be relieved when the surgery was over and I had been reassured that it had not spread further, but my eternal hopefulness was not so much dented as it would have been for many.

In the next few days, I had to share this first with immediate family, and then with friends and colleagues. With my typical sense of humor, I commented soon on what a showstopper this was. The news that one had cancer stopped anyone expecting anything of you — quite a relief in some ways, and it made me laugh. Perhaps a part of my laughter was that false sense of invulnerability all of us have, but part of it too was a healthy, continued ability to laugh at the ups and downs of life, which a high school course in mental health had long ago defined as emotional maturity.

Surgery was less than two weeks away, for which I was glad. I had a healthy fear of the cancer spreading, and wanted it out as soon as possible. But I was ambivalent about saying goodbye to a vital organ that had served me well for 66 years. It also seemed a little crazy to me, as I continued to feel tip-top and high energy, to make myself so sick as major surgery would do, when outwardly I was just fine. I had some normal dread of post-surgery pain and incapacitation, and the sense that once I got into the hospital, things would be out of my control. On the other hand, I felt very good that all my experiences with this hospital, Branson, had been excellent, so if I had to be in someone else's hands, Branson was a good place to have me.

On the day of the surgery, there was some confusion about where operative patients were supposed to go, as a result of which several of us were waiting in one place while the nurse who had to prepare us was waiting more and more anxiously in another. She was obviously upset by this, trying hard not to bawl out a pre-operative patient, but needing to vent somewhere, so when I arrived in the theatre outside the surgery room, I found myself apologizing to Dr. Noakes for our being a few minutes late. He smiled serenely, and murmured, "What's to be worried about? You're here, I'm here, the rest of the team is here, and we're ready to go." He went on introducing me with complete respect, as if we were at a formal gathering, to the team that would help him. That kindness and inclusivity extended to the operating room itself, where a nurse remembered to explain a potentially scary term just as I was passing out under the anesthetic.

I need not go into a blow-by-blow account of "my operation." Things went well, Branson lived up to its previous performance, and Dr. Noakes assured me that the operation had been successful and the prognosis was good. I experienced a floral display of community support that was quite overwhelming — I joked about my political section, as my community work had linked me with local politicians so much that each of them had sent me a beautiful bouquet. Both in the hospital and afterwards, I was feted with cards, letters, and visits, and I found the month of recuperation at home thoroughly enjoyable. I was in little pain, getting stronger every day, and despite the callers, had time to sit in my easy chair, smell the aroma of the flowers, and catch up on wonderful reading.

The one scary note in all this period was that I saw a brochure when I went back for my first quarterly checkup, about "cancer recurrence." Easy as my brush had been, the thought of recurrence was horrifying to me. I spent a few moments empathizing with those who went through such a horror show, but prayed confidently that I would be spared such an experience. My understanding of the doctor's prediction was that I was fairly safe. Kidney cancer of my type, size, and location had only about a ten percent chance of recurring. Because of its location, deep inside, neither radiation nor chemotherapy was recommended to prevent relapse, so the good news was that I would not have to suffer through either of these treatments, which many people felt were almost as bad as the disease. The bad news was that, because of the impenetrability of this area of the body, if the cancer did recur, there was little that could be done for it. But since I didn't expect recurrence, and since the odds were ten to one in my favor, I joked about having the best of both worlds: a simple operation and neither chemotherapy nor radiation.

As the year went on, my customary resilience reasserted itself. The operation left a few digestive rumblings for a month or so, but these gradually died down as the organs sorted themselves out with my left kidney missing. As promised, the right kidney demonstrated that it could do the whole work of both, and I would not have known I was missing anything. My three-month checkup was fine, my six-month checkup was fine, and each time I gained further confidence.

In the spring, however, I began to have digestive rumblings again. Spicy foods, cream, things with lots of tomato, left me with lots of wind. It felt like a recurrence of colitis, which I had had once in my life, years before, after a period of great stress. I treated it like colitis, and a mild diet, plenty of walking and bland whole grains seemed to help it. I consulted the doctor who agreed with me that it was probably irritable bowel, a variation on the colitis idea. But every time I thought I was finally getting over it, it would come back again.

This was the situation in May 2000, when I had my final ultrasound checkup for the year, after which I was to go to annual checks. As with the original diagnostic ultrasound, the technician called in his superior and the two of them talked away incomprehensibly about it. When they told me to go without saying anything more, I asked what that was about, but the technician said it was just a bit of my bowel he had misread as something else.

From May 10 to 13 we held the Ninth International Conference on Penal Abolition (ICOPA) in Toronto, one of the biggest organizing events of my life. We had brought 450 people from 22 countries, we included Africa and Asia for the first time, we had simultaneous translation into both French and Spanish, and we had subsidized everyone who had asked for a subsidy, thus the conference was about half comprised of low-income people. We hadn't just talked about crashing the social class barrier, we had done it! We had also linked the issues of corporate rule and corporate crime with that of penal abolition and had exposed the racism and classism that are the hallmark of our criminal injustice system everywhere in today's world.

I was chair of the organizing committee, spoke on several panels, and was generally in the center of the storm of dynamic energy at ICOPA IX. I brought along some easy-to-digest food and managed it all. Nine days after it was over, we were due for a long postponed visit to see our grandchildren in England — little Pippa had been born the previous fall and we had not yet met, as I couldn't take that much time off from organizing the conference. So we went for three weeks to relax, visit several relatives there, and recuperate from the conference.

The problem was, the pain in my digestive system became rapidly more acute, and my chronically weak back began acting up too. Each week I withdrew more and more from the little family trips and events, and kept saying, "I have to rest some and try to get my back and digestion back in shape." In the last week I even went to a British doctor, and considered coming back early to get to the bottom of the situation. By the time we did get back, I rushed to my general practitioner who agreed with me that the situation was serious. By this time I was on round-the-clock Tylenol, but I was scheduled for a CT-scan on Wednesday, June 21, and both the surgeon and GP were confident this would reveal the problem.

Meanwhile, I was beginning a week of farewell celebrations, because my husband and I were planning to move west in the fall of 2000, following our May retirements, to relieve his emphysema with the healthier air of Salmon Arm, British Columbia. We had lived in Toronto for thirty years and our many friends, colleagues, and acquaintances wanted to wish us well. I had four events to go to that week, the biggest of which was a huge community event in Jane-Finch, the neighborhood where we had lived for all those years and where I had worked to support our strong community for ten years. This event took place on Monday, June 19th, and I had to take Tylenols, every two hours, throughout the entire day.

Yet the event itself was wonderful. Both local councilors, who had a highly competitive relationship, agreed to work together on the event, a favor I had asked of them, and they jointly presented me with a lovely plaque with these words:

> Mayor Mel Lastman and Members of Toronto City Council extend congratulations and appreciation to Ruth Morris . . . You have spoken and written about justice, and acted with courage and passion on various issues. You have shared your vision of creating community by building on the strengths of all regardless of race, creed or economic standing... As you leave the community, which has been your home for more than three decades... may the wonderful memories and joyous melodies of your life find new ways to nurture you...

It is somewhat embarrassing to print out this tribute but I think it is relevant because from time to time in this book I have spoken of my work traumas, which happened to me because of the very same behaviors that were now being praised. When you take a stand it is important to recognize that while many criticize you, others admire you all the more for every arrow shot at you. Even many of your critics grudgingly admire your courage and vision and integrity. At any rate, it was a beautiful evening, with many moving personal tributes and scores of personal exchanges that meant so much to us.

It was a rude contrast to go to the CT-scan a day and a half later, struggling to keep down cups of the unpleasant barium, doubly hard to hold down because of the digestive symptoms that were becoming rapidly worse. But I managed it, and the CT-scan was taken in the morning of the 21st. That afternoon at about three p.m., the GP phoned and asked us to come in to see him. I knew that such a quick summons to his office with no, "Don't worry!" was not good news, but I had no idea how bad it was going to be. Where the left kidney had been removed, a new tumor had grown, larger than the first, and so near the aorta that they could not operate. They referred me to a specialist at Princess Margaret Hospital, which specializes in cancer, about possible chemotherapy, but at best it could only slow things down, not cure them. The GP declined to project my life expectancy, saying it varied a lot, but I wondered how far I would be able to be functional for any of it. I was afraid of the amount of pain ahead, but prayed for strength to deal with it.

Of course the worst part was that Ray and I were very sad at our coming separation, and shed many tears over that.

Shock had carried me through that first day. At first, Ray and I just sat around, totally exhausted, trying to take it in, while wanting not to. We cried a little, we talked a little, but a lot of the time we just sat there, metaphorically gasping for air. We couldn't do that for long, as we were due to go out in two more hours to the Annual General Meeting of a local group whose founding I had assisted, which wanted to present me with an award of recognition. Much as I believe in sharing things openly with people, this was not an occasion to announce or even to share privately this bombshell. So we went, sat around and chatted, listened to the award, and I even made a normal little speech of appreciation for the organization and gave thanks for the award. I was proud that no one guessed what we were processing, but I also knew that shock was carrying us through that first evening.

Yet by itself shock could not have done it — the hard homework described in this book had enabled me to process grief, had given me practice at it, and had shown me the steps forward. More important still, my relationship to God was practiced, and so it was there to strengthen me when I most needed it. Did it make it easy? Of course not — but it made it possible.

The other strange thing that prepared me, I discovered, was having grown through earlier traumas, especially my two firings and that grueling inquest. In all those situations I had to make farewell talks to groups when I was brutally under fire, some of them friendly, some not at all, some in between. I learned how to bid farewell with grace, I think, thanks to God's grace, in hard situations. So in *some* ways this one was a piece of cake, because unlike those times, there was no shadow of anyone blaming me for being fired from life. This time I knew that when I told people this news, I would get back nothing but sympathy and support.

After the meeting with our GP, Ray and I shifted from a complete expectation of ongoing life for me to complete acceptance of a short life span. Within two days, the yo-yo effect began on this issue of life and death. I talked to our surgeon, and he gave us back the gift of hope. When Dr. Noakes was sure we understood the seriousness of the situation, his tone and voice changed to one of hope and energy. I had been thanking him for all he had done, and he started to say, "It's been a pleasure knowing and working with you too." Then he switched to a very positive voice, and said, "And it *will* be too, because we're not giving up on this. This doctor at Princess Margaret is a miracle worker — I have seen her put very advanced cancers into total remission, and we're going to fight this thing all the way!" So that gave us a bit of hope to hang our hats on.

We decided to postpone our plans to move to Salmon Arm in September, since we needed to prioritize my chemotherapy here, and we were unsure if I would be strong enough in the fall for a move.

My eldest daughter Corinne was planning a major visit with her two young children. My niece Laurie was paying for a consultation with an expert who had healed his own cancer with holistic nutrition. Our son Peter offered to donate one of his own kidneys if that would help. Each of our other family members reached out in several ways.

The next utterly heartwarming surprise was an amazing letter from our daughter Joy, who called it "my everything-I-don't-want-not-to-have-said letter," and who took several days to compose it carefully. I include part of it here because it is a reminder of how valuable to both parties such a message is while a loved one is still in this sphere of life. One of the biggest blocks to recovering from bereavement is the feeling that we never told our loved one clearly enough how much we loved them. Joy's letter is a wonderful insurance against such hard grief:

Thank you so much for all that you have meant to me all my life. You have been a model for me, a friend I could always rely on, a mainstay of my existence. Always there, loving me, ready to support me . . . For me you are, of course, the definition of mother, and mother is a beautiful word.

One of the things I will always remember about my childhood and what made it so good is "special time." There was always that time for each of us, for whatever we wanted to do, sometimes even full days — almost like extra birthdays, except that of course on birthdays the whole family participated in our chosen activities. I tell people about special time sometimes, when I talk about my childhood and what made it good. That is one thing, but there were so many ways in which you made my childhood a wonderful, carefree time: bedtime reading; stories and songs; homemade games; letting me help in the kitchen; teaching me to sew; planning fun family vacations; music; card games; family worship; your volunteer work in my schools... So many of my friends who talk about their childhoods describe them as incredibly poor in relation to mine, so I know how lucky I am to have you. You respected my terror of hurdles, and were willing to protect me by talking to Mrs. Green before Grade 2 started, and making sure that I wouldn't be made to do them. You helped me find and settle into ALP, and took me away from my last week of Grade 3 after Sandy terrorized me. I could always count on you.

You've also taught me a lot about courage. I've only really started to realize recently how much courage it would take to invite a relative stranger to stay in your home. Not only near strangers, but ex-convicts, when you had young children. That takes a great deal of both courage and faith, in ways I'm only now beginning to understand — because of course, at the time, it seemed perfectly natural. Only now do I realize that I wouldn't invite a homeless person home with me under most circumstances. I can't live up to all that you've taught me, but you have set the example.

You've taught me a value system that you haven't just mouthed, but consistently lived up to. I grew up marching in demos, really understanding that there was more to the world than things that happened to directly impact my life. I remember as a child, proudly coming up with the idea of socialism – "Why aren't there free stores?" I asked you this, not realizing that this was not a new concept, but simply seeing it as a method of eliminating irrational social hierarchies — a natural part of true social justice as you'd helped me see it.

There is so much you've done for me, given me, taught me over the years; I couldn't even begin to list most of it. Suffice it to say that a big part of who I am is very directly your influence. Part of you will always be a part of me, just as G-ma has been so much a part of you that a part of her has been passed on, through you, to us. I don't know that I've ever thanked you for all you've been and done — it never seemed to need to be said, but thank you. I've always been proud to introduce you to my friends as my mother, something I'm not sure many children would say of their own mothers.

This is not to say you don't have faults. I no longer believe that "My Mommy is perfect" — but for me, you have always been a wonderful mother. ...There's a large part of me desperately trying to retreat to the days when Mommy could do anything and just say, "Mommy, it hurts. Make it better!" Sadly I've grown past thinking that you can do that. Instead, I'm sitting in a mountain meadow, listening to birds and insects, praying, and writing this letter, because I don't want to have regrets later about things I never said.

Love always, Joy

Once again, I have mixed feelings about sharing the warmth and beauty of this very personal letter. But my life has always stood for the risks of sharing our vulnerability and our truth wherever they can help others. Joy's letter has the recipe for saying the things that so much need to be said.

Significantly, Joy's references to my protecting her from childhood fears are reminders that protecting children when they are small helps them to grow strong enough to face the challenges and traumas of adulthood with complete confidence. Children need not confront all their fears alone to overcome them; sometimes they need their parents to tackle the fear on their behalf. This teaches them both that it is possible to confront fear and that standing up for someone else is a virtue. In adulthood Joy has repeatedly confronted the governments of Canada and her university officials on the rights of students to respect and affordable education. She has walked in the great demonstrations of our time, and has shown every type of courage as an adult, for which those little bits of childhood protection prepared her.

One of the most important messages of that letter is how much parents of adult children need to hear such positive memories. Among the hard lettings go of life, learning to let go successively of babyhood, toddler ways, kindergarten adventures, school days, adolescent struggles, and then the struggles of adult children are surely among the hardest. It is wonderful when children can affirm their parents for all that in the way Joy did, and I can never read her words without tears of joy and thankfulness. I put more into my career as mother than any other career, and it is so good to know that our children experienced fulfillment through it. I wrote her an answer, but I shall save that for later.

Summer: Surrounded by Love and Support

> That day which you fear as being the end of all things
> Is the birthday of your eternity.
>
> — SENECA

One of the things I discovered early on was that it did not work well to tell this news over the phone or in person, if it was possible to send a letter first. People were so shocked that they were struggling with their own feelings, and they needed time to regroup in order to think about what they wanted to say to me. Many of them coped very well, but it was stressful, for both me and the hearer, for me to spill it all in a direct communication. A letter could prepare the way for a more considered response, and give the hearer time to digest some of their own pain before they had to deal with my feelings and needs. Nevertheless, I continued on my lifelong path of sharing the most important things in my life quite openly with a wide circle of family and friends. Yet I found that trying to write out the news and my own feelings about it over and over, individually, was both time-consuming and wearing.

So on July 8th I sent a "group letter" that summed up the medical information and our responses to it at that point. The first page summed up the history of the disease, and its interaction with major events in my life such as the Conference and the visit to our grandchildren in England. The second page stated the irony of the various community "farewells to Ruth Morris" at a time when a much bigger farewell was shadowing us. I summed up the cancer specialist's opinion: that I had only a sixty percent chance of any improvement from the chemotherapy, and only a four to ten percent chance of enough reduction of the tumor to contribute to a real cure. But I also pointed out that the statistics of medical science did not hold all the answers. Naturopathy, diet, Chinese herbal supports, and above all, the power of prayer, were still to be explored:

> How much difference it makes knowing that a community of loving friends, as well as others who do not even know me directly, are holding me in a worldwide network of prayer through all this and all that is to come. Thank you, thank you, thank you — believers and unbelievers, prayer can only help both you and me. God takes our offerings from where we are, and each of you can help me, and one another, by joining this beautiful community, which I feel as tangibly as I have ever felt anything.
>
> So make your prayers prayers of hope that all things are possible. In praying about this I am reminded of a wonderful book by someone who communicated lovingly with all forms of life, and even wrote a

letter to a colony of ants living in his kitchen. He explained to them that they had their place and he had his, and that he loved them, but his kitchen was not the place for them, and would they move out by tomorrow afternoon? And they did! I feel like that about the cancer cells in my body. Cancer is a part of God's world, and these cells are following some guidance that is off target for the needs of my whole body. Please write them a spiritual letter with me, respecting them too as part of God's creation, but asking them to move out and respect the needs of their host.

I was practicing here two of the basic rules for helping friends to give us what we need in times of trauma: we have to ask as concretely as possible for precisely what we need, and make those requests something they can deliver. I acknowledged the fact that my friends had varying degrees and kinds of faith, but that every one could pray for me in some sense; my agnostic friends were deeply touched that I valued their prayers, too. Secondly, we need to validate the efforts people are making – both the nearby friends and the distant ones praying for me – with deep and sincere gratitude.

But July brought yet another shock. We came home one day to a message I could not believe. My brother Dave, who was just 5 years older than me and had been in perfect health, had gone for his morning bike ride, laid down for a nap before lunch, and never woken up. He had come up to visit me — from Buffalo to Toronto — shortly before, and had phoned to express his support about three days before he died. At first, I just kept exclaiming that this could not be real, that I could not, *would* not believe it. But of course it was real, and I was still too ill to go down to Buffalo for the funeral. My husband and two of our children did go, though, and Ray read my three-page eulogy to Dave.

In a strange way I had an eerie suspicion that if Dave had any choice in his hasty passage, he would have wanted to get over there so that he could prepare a proper welcoming committee for his little sister. Despite my shock and grief, I felt a certain comfort that the brother closest to me in age was waiting in the wings to cheer when I passed over, and heaven looked even more welcoming than it had before. Still, there was the normal grief to go through, and I would think about how we had always harmonized hymns and religious songs together, and could never do it again in this world. I was deeply grateful that Ray, Doug, and Joy could go and represent us, and bring back the experience of the memorial service to make it more real for me.

It was in July also that our local councilor, Peter LiPreti, had hand delivered to my home a beautiful plaque that not only paid tribute to the qualities he had seen in me, but which pledged to create an award in my name for two students, for the next ten years, who most effectively demonstrated commitment to promoting justice, being peacemakers, and doing loving acts of kindness. When Peter first proposed this to me, I was so stunned and overwhelmed I just cried, and now he had made it a reality.

By August we were able to establish a prayer group in our home, which came every other week to do laying on of hands prayer for me. Since Anglicans are particularly strong in preserving the faith-healing tradition of Christianity, we consulted an Anglican expert on the format, and then gradually worked out our own. With each session we began with checking in on how we were, and I especially shared a little about how things were going for me. Then we had fifteen minutes of centering prayer, followed by fifteen minutes in which people gathered around me, put their hands on me, and prayed for my health and our well being as a family. Finally, we returned to the circle and debriefed, sharing how the session had been for each of us. We usually had light refreshments at the start or finish, and the whole session was about an hour and a half.

The prayer group was, again, a good example of asking for what you need. Many people offered to help without knowing what to do, so I took the liberty of approaching some of them, and some others who had not specifically offered but whom I felt confident would want to help. I asked several people from our Friends Meeting and an equal number from the community where we lived and where I had worked for ten years. The result was a group of about six regulars outside of Ray and me, with others coming sporadically. I had been unsure how it would work out, never having been part of such a group before. I knew it was an imposition on everyone's time and a long trip for the downtowners, and I realized that the two groups did not know each other. Nevertheless, after a couple of tentative sessions, the group jelled, and we went from strength to strength. Most members said repeatedly that the experience was wonderful for them, and we were of course deeply grateful for this concrete caring and support.

Not a week went by that summer without some beautiful bouquet of flowers, and most weeks there were several. Cards and calls came in abundance, and e-mails and other letters flowed in daily. Close friends offered help with transport, housecleaning, recovery ideas, expert resources, books, tapes, Reiki. In fact, in many ways this experience refutes the thesis of this book: that most friends in our culture want to help those in trauma but don't know how. Mine certainly did know how. In fact, it has been the support and love from my friends that has taught me to write this book, far more so than my having undergone the traumas themselves.

Years ago, when my wonderful mother was slowly dying of Alzheimer's disease, I said I would rather die of cancer, but I had never expected to have my offer taken up in this way. Both of these forms of passing have the disadvantage of a long, slow look at the process and reality of our own deaths, and cancer carries with it full awareness. It is often said that a quick passage from an overwhelming heart attack, quiet death in a single night, or a sudden fatal accident, is harder on the relatives but easier on the deceased. Yet, the messages of support that kept coming in made me aware of one advantage of a slow journey toward possible death: one's friends have plenty of opportunities to say, in many different words, things that often remain unsaid. How often had I signed cards at some gathering for absent friends who were prevented from participating by illness or other life events? Now I received such loving cards, each with so many messages and signatures.

Every one of us has friends to whom we have meant much. Yet I was startled by the number of people, including people my age and older, who said that in some way my life had inspired them.

On August 20th my editor and friend, Ruth Bradley-St-Cyr, asked me to attend her church where she was preaching. I came to support her, and was overwhelmed when the sermon used my life and United Church missionary Dr. Robert McClure's life as different examples of our call to service in this world. By being faithful to our own dreams, and supportive to one another, Ruth and I had built a relationship that we pledged to continue even beyond my eventual death. As Ruth said in her sermon: "our two types of missionary activity have intertwined and strengthened each other – my edit-ing and her activism." Our working relationship just seemed meant to be.

The first book that Ruth and I worked on together, *Stories of Transformative Justice*, shares many lessons of how life-changing justice can be when it is not based on revenge. I did much work for penal abolition and transformative justice throughout my life, whether I was paid to do it or not. Some years ago Ray and I also launched a not-for-profit organization called Rittenhouse (my maiden name) to promote transformative justice. This work is being done throughout the world and so I have colleagues worldwide, many of them gleaned through the biannual International Conference on Penal Abolition. One colleague from New Zealand wrote:

> You have inspired me... You have always faced life with a strong pur-pose — to free the captured, promote justice, and send a message of love to everyone... At times when I felt particularly alone in the work, I have thought of the struggles you had to be heard, to be recognized and to continue. I knew I was never alone in the battle. You and Ray are my idea of what true Quakerism is about... your ability to stay on the cutting edge... You have always had a genius for leading people to the place in the light that met their needs wherever they were, and then helping them to find it for themselves.

One of the most awesome gifts that summer came from my friend Pat Moles, who had been one of our closest friends in our years in Washington, D.C. In the thirty years since then, we had drifted apart and barely exchanged Christmas letters. But now, when the chips were down, it was as if our friendship had never lost any of its intensity. Pat wrote me in July:

> I have your July 8th letter within reach throughout every day, and rereading it is a comfort and a gift to me, as it must be for all who received it. Everything you wrote helps to strengthen my prayers for you and Ray, and increases my hope that the burden of this illness will be fully lifted from your body.
>
> By the time I had gotten to the beautiful words you wrote about living in a spiritual reality, I saw that you used the words from Fra

Giovanni – "You touch the Angel's hand that brings it to you." I realized that, of course, you have the words from that letter in your heart. I have had it word for word as a part of me always, along with gratitude for your gift of it to me.

I want to give you the original (I have made many copies) so you can hold it as I have held it so often as a reminder of all the strength and inspiration you have given to others.

With this letter, she enclosed the original of the Fra Giovanni card, which I had given her so many years ago. She wanted me to absorb all the tears and joys whose spirit had penetrated to the very fiber of that precious card, so that when I touched it, I could touch the spirit of our friendship, and the spirit of our journey in this world together. I still cannot write of this gift without tears.

I also received a unique letter from my last student, Leonard Molczadski, whose father had lost much of his family in the Holocaust. Leonard is one of the most spiritually profound young people I have known; his letter carried me with him to that spiritual realm:

Yesterday I watched the most beautiful sunset behind the mountains that surround this city. Suddenly I saw this beauty before me as a metaphor for life. As the sun's brilliant light grew dimmer and dimmer my eyes focused on the majestic trees atop the mountains. For me those trees represent the lives potentially enriched by one soul. As darkness increased, I continued to focus on those beautiful trees.

Walking home I thought of you, Ruth. When you cross the great divide there will be a profound darkness at your physical loss. I believe that eventually a new day will dawn for those of us whose lives have been enriched with wisdom, compassion and love. In this sense, Ruth, you will be very much with us. You will be our sun, and we will be your majestic trees, standing proudly atop the mountain of life waiting to receive your lights of social justice. I smiled all the way home last night, because I realized death is not an ending, but rather a continuation.

Each of us has been a sun to someone in this life, and our witness goes on in this world, while we ourselves take our graduated spirits to the next realm of adventure and building.

The Waiting Room

Have courage for the great sorrows of life
And patience for the small ones,
And when you have laboriously accomplished your daily task,
Go to sleep in peace. God is awake.

— VICTOR HUGO

The wonderful caring spirit of Princess Margaret Hospital in general, and of the chemo daycare unit in particular, was evident from my first chemotherapy treatment. The nurses did everything possible to make a scary, unpleasant experience a warm, friendly, safe, comfortable one. I was surrounded by love at every level. Ray and my life-long friend Margie carried me on the shoulders of their faithful love — 40 and 50 years of devotion — and the nurses and patients provided a culture of caring I have seldom experienced anywhere. With each moment of immersion in it, my spirits soared. These chemotherapy sessions became weekly adventures.

Years ago I read a pamphlet by Leslie Weatherhead on "The Will of God." In it he argued that the *ideal* will of God is always for healing, wholeness and safety for all. But for reasons that none of us can fully grasp intellectually, God allows a world where accidents, disease, disaster, and our own neglect of compassion bring about much suffering. In those circumstances, the *circumstantial* will of God is that we make as much good as possible come out of these evils, turning "irritation into iridescence," as my mother used to say. Over the years, I have noted that although theologians, philosophers, and plain folks differed widely in accounting for evil in this world, they agreed almost unanimously on the conclusion that we are meant to use adversity to create a better world.

I found Princess Margaret Hospital's chemotherapy daycare department a wonderful opportunity to do just that. Every patient and relative of a patient in it was suffering. Every staff person was part of a team dedicated to bringing love, cheer, and caring into that suffering. Helen, a receptionist who brought so much individual care, listening, joy and love into each day, especially awed me. She taught me again that putting positive energy into a job could re-energize us as we go. Helen was like a hostess at a party that no one wanted to come to, determined to help everyone have a good time. Helen ran on high gear all day long, reaching out with extra gestures, responding to every inquiry, explaining things lovingly, and yet she obviously went home walking on air, taking great pleasure in doing an important job superbly. So it was fertile soil indeed for someone like me to seek God's will each week, adding my little bit of healing to someone, even if it was usually only by caring listening. I came across a powerful thought in one book, to the effect that the real tragedy of cancer is not to die from it, but to miss the life lessons we are meant to learn from it. So I tried, each day and each week, to do my homework.

One week a family group came into the waiting room, and I puzzled over who was the patient and where they all fit in. There were two adult women, a teenage boy, and two girls. One of the adult women was walking with a cane and had a totally bald head, so she was obviously a strong candidate for the patient role. The bigger of the girls seemed to be a healthy teenager like the boy but the littler girl was the mystery. She was the size of a ten-year-old child, with the voice of a child, but she had fully developed breasts, and was dressed more like a teen. She was also bald on most of her head, with just a tiny bit of fluff made into two tiny braids on the back of her head. It was unclear whether she was a patient there as well. In general, children were served by Sick Children's Hospital.

I watched them discreetly with interest and, by luck, they went for treatment in the chair right next to ours, so we got to know them very well. Crystal, the little girl, was very friendly and chatty, and so were they all. It turned out the healthy adult woman was the sister of the bald woman, who was the patient. The teen boy was the son of the healthy sister. The two girls were actually identical twins, fourteen years old, and the daughters of the women getting treatment. What a story lay behind that!

When the twins were born, the one who now looks healthy almost died from a series of non-malignant tumors all over her tongue. She had a series of operations, in the course of which she lost half her tongue, and had to relearn to talk after each operation. She never had speech therapy, yet amazingly she speaks almost fully normally. Not long after she recovered from her last tongue surgery, when the twins were six, Crystal developed severe malignant brain tumors. She was not expected to live, and got one of those trips from the Children's Wish Foundation, but Sick Children's Hospital blasted her with every bit of radiation and chemotherapy they could. Although she suffered severe burns from it, as well as stunted growth and permanent loss of hair, she just glowed when she said she had been in remission for seven years now. She was also very proud to show us her crocheting and tell us about other crafts she makes for sale.

Not long after Crystal went into remission, their mother developed breast cancer. When that was gone, she had a relapse in her lungs. They took out part of one lung, and she was all right for a bit, but it had now spread to her hip, and a bit more in her lung, which sounded ominous to me. Yet there they were, together as a family – cheerful, and somehow coping with a life that had been one calamity after another for fourteen years. The mother is so sick after each chemotherapy treatment that her sister and nephew come to stay with them for a week to take care of them. Amazingly enough, the girls' dad is still hanging in there through all this, and was going to meet their train when they finally got home.

All three of the children were not like average teens, in the sense that they were very warm, outgoing, and trusting toward adults like Ray and me. It was as if life had jolted them out of all that superficial stuff and they realized we are all allies in the great struggles of this world. There was so much to hear from them that I never thought about telling them anything of our situation, something I generally share freely. I was very touched by their farewell, when they finished before we did. Crystal came over and kissed me, and we all shook hands. Crystal's aunt looked at me with tears in her eyes and just said very movingly, "Be well, be well."

Somehow, I never got around to asking them how they coped with it all. It must have been a remarkable faith journey as well as a journey in family support. Obviously, as the nurse and I were saying after they had left, there is also either a severe hereditary problem, or more likely an environmental factor such as pollution or radiation. But such worldly true explanations still leave so much to deal with spiritually: the old question of how a just and caring and powerful God can let corporations and people do these things to one another in the name of maximizing profit and "growth." The nurse also spoke of another mother and daughter they had treated for a variety of cancers — they lived ten miles from Chernobyl at the time of the catastrophe there. Ever since, I think of Crystal's family with warmth, and send prayers for their physical healing and spiritual strength.

The young couples also amazed me. One day a young woman came in. She made up one of the beds, then climbed in, and obviously exhausted, went to sleep. Then her husband arrived, and he sat by the bed, just whispering to her from time to time, and holding her hand and cuddling up to her. She alternately responded or just lay there, worn out. I saw quite a few of these young couples, and I thought how horrible it would be to try to cope with this experience early in one's marriage, when life was just opening up.

At the community farewell in June, bridge-building had been one of three key phrases that kept recurring about me — passion and social justice were the other two. The videos about chemotherapy had impressed me with how this disease builds a bridge of the community of suffering across rich and poor, black and white, left and right, those with faith and those without. So cancer offered me yet another field of bridges to explore.

I wished I could share with the world what that waiting room did for me: making me realize each day more clearly how precious is the gift of every well moment, which we too often want to "get through," instead of valuing for the precious gift it is. I was also impressed by the amount of strong family support I saw there. Almost no one came alone, and the unit encouraged groups of people to come and be with the patient through the whole treatment. They also offered drinks and Popsicles, partly to get more liquid into patients, but mainly, I felt, just to add a friendly touch to it all.

Experiencing that waiting room was like a pilgrimage into the deeper mysteries of life. I found those days exhausting, and it wasn't just the long wait and the treatment itself. The exhaustion was from being plunged so deeply into the school of human suffering, and sharing it with new strangers each time. Yet these strangers were no longer strangers at each day's end, but neighbors in the great journey of suffering.

CHAPTER 8

Forgiveness, Healing, and Reintegration

That man has no need to forget who knows what forgiveness is.
— EMIL FUCHS, *Christ in Catastrophe*

B EFORE WE CAN FULLY REINTEGRATE, we need to tackle the hard
issue of forgiveness at its roots. Even more than most steps along the
healing road, forgiveness is a long and gradual journey. The path is challenging, and it is not a steady uphill climb. Like most growing in this life, it
is two steps forward, a hole to stumble in, a step down, a stone to go
around, and then another step forward. Sometimes we are disappointed
when we think we have mastered it, and find anger and even the gut-
wrenching threat of hatred gripping us again. But we must never forget it is
a process: a slow and gradual one, an act of will, not a miraculous feeling of
love and goodwill that never goes away. That is why we have talked about
parts of that process in each stage: letting go, trying to love the opposition
in theory, and now, in reintegration, when it is time to look the issue of forgiveness full in the face.

Marietta Jaeger practices what she calls her "gospel of forgiveness," and
few have been given tougher challenges. Her seven-year-old daughter Susie
was kidnapped on a family camping trip and killed by pedophile and serial
killer named David:

I believe God allowed Susie to be taken from us — and I don't understand all the reasons why. But I know He has redeemed her death over

and over. By giving me the ability to forgive David, to come away from the experience with a sense of peace and a feeling of great love for God. It was Susie's death that led police to David so he wasn't able to kill any more children. Many people tell me they've been touched by my story, that they've been able to forgive someone in their life who has hurt them. And I believe God will continue to show me the good that can come out of Susie's death.

Wilma Dirksen, whose daughter was murdered, has participated in a number of victims' groups, and this loving Mennonite smilingly says, "Victims groups call forgiveness the f—' word." That is because we ram it down their throats in early shock and grief, without acknowledging the wrong they have experienced, without giving them time to vent their natural anger, violation, fear, and anguish. It is wrong to expect victims to arrive magically at the mountaintop of full forgiveness immediately after a major trauma. Grief work is a climb, and we cannot arrive at the pinnacle without a long period of setting one foot before the other, climbing up that mountain. But now, in reintegration, we have come a long way, and the lingering unresolved feelings toward those who have wronged us are part of what holds us back. It is time to look forgiveness full in the face.

Building A New Life

> The child cries out when from the right breast the mother takes it away, in the very next moment to find in the left one its consolation.
>
> — RABINDARANATH TAGORE

Three critical issues must be dealt with as we move forward into healing and reintegration: forgiveness, learning to risk love and trust again, and accepting failure.

Forgiveness

> To err is human; to forgive, divine.
>
> — ALEXANDER POPE, *An Essay on Criticism*

Forgiveness is never easy, but it is hardest when we have to go on coping daily with the person who has hurt us, when the world fails to acknowledge our wrong, and when the wrongs continue. Some years ago, the Pope visited in prison the man who had tried to kill him. Beautiful as that act by the Pope was, it was not as hard as some of the challenges given to humbler people. The world fully acknowledges the great wrong that man did to the Pope, and the Pope never has to see him again unless he chooses. But the situation of a wife whose brilliant, charming, and successful husband is emotionally cruel to her is just the opposite. She has to cope day after day with a situation where neither her husband nor the world gives her any support in the daily heroic struggle she wages to forgive her continuing hurts.

However hard or easy forgiveness is in theory, it almost always takes a strong act of will to move ourselves into it. I say almost always, because occasionally I have been granted forgiveness toward someone who has hurt me as a free gift of grace; it is a mystery when and why it comes, but we cannot count on such dispensations.

One of the most important lessons we have to learn in forgiveness is that we cannot control the response of the object of our forgiveness. However perfectly we play our part, we cannot by the purity of our spirit prevent our offering being thrown back in our faces. It is a hard lesson to learn that the only person we can change by our own will is ourselves. We have to surrender all the other actors to God's care, not our personal salvation.

However, I don't believe we can start by trying to forgive the other party. There are three parties to forgive. There is no exact moment when we move from one to another, but to some extent we have to forgive these parties in sequence:

First, we have to forgive ourselves.

Secondly, audacious or sacrilegious as it may sound, we have to forgive God for allowing a world where these kinds of things can happen.

Finally, when we have dealt with those two big hurdles, we are a little more nearly ready to face the enormous challenge of forgiving the person or persons who have hurt us.

FORGIVING YOURSELF

Forgiving yourself is the *if-only* stage. This is when you replay the thing again and again and again in your mind. If only I had left the house a minute earlier or later. If only I had never taken that rotten job. If only I had never invited him or her to my house. The *if-onlys* can go on forever.

One summer when I was in the depths of a bad trauma, I went to hear a handicapped Vietnam veteran talk about success. Although he had lost three limbs in a catastrophe in Vietnam, he was now a U.S. Congressman with wonderful achievements. He talked about how he had spent the best part of a year replaying the 30-second script of how he had stepped on that land mine. He tried walking around it; he tried looking, and seeing some sign of it. He tried imagining some other poor soul stepping on it first — why me?! He got out of it in dozens of different ways in his mind's eye. But all those replays accomplished were to bog him down, as long as he remained absorbed in them. The most important words he said that day were, "Finally, I made up my mind that I would never accomplish anything in my life until I quit replaying that 30-second scenario, and got on with it."

That's the most important step in forgiving yourself: quit replaying your particular 30-second scenario, or 3-month scenario, or whatever it is. By all means learn from your mistakes. But don't destroy your usefulness by berating yourself endlessly for the past. When you have learned what you can from your real mistakes, let them go, forgive yourself, and move on. Equally important, don't keep berating yourself for choices whose ills you could not possibly have foreseen, no matter how many times you replay them now. God does not give us divine foresight into future events. There comes a time too when we need to leave the past in God's hands.

The *if-only* stage *is* a necessary stage. We have to learn what we can from it, to avert similar tragedies in the future. But it is far too easy to get stuck in it long after we have learned all we can. That's when we have to have the decency to forgive ourselves and move on. We also have to accept our right to all our emotions: anger, hurt, pain and grief. They're all normal, and we need to allow ourselves to feel them.

Years ago a wonderful psychiatrist gave one of our children a button to wear, which contained an unforgettable piece of wisdom. It proudly proclaimed: "I *have the courage to be imperfect!*" Having learned what we can from our mistakes, we too must go forward in life, head high, seeking to improve, but always having the courage to be imperfect. Accepting our own right to imperfection is one of the most essential steps in the risk of ongoing creative living, and it includes the full and free forgiveness of ourselves.

Forgiving God

Once we are ready to move beyond our replays and *if-onlys*, and truly forgive ourselves, we then face the incredible challenge of forgiving God. That sounds like a terrible thing to say. But, whether we like it or not, we all face the challenge of forgiving God at some point in our spiritual journey, and most of us have to wrestle with it many times. It only makes it harder when we won't admit we are fighting that battle within ourselves.

One of my favorite saints is Saint Teresa of Avila, because she had such a great sense of humor. She also had a beautiful intimacy with God, and used to have her own fireside chats with God, in which they talked very frankly. The absolute trust between them was expressed in her beautiful words:

Let nothing disturb thee, let nothing affright thee.
All things are passing. God never changes.
Patience gains all things.
Who has God wants nothing.
God alone suffices.

At the other extreme, she could wryly share a joke with God and frequently did. One day she commented critically to God, "Lord, if I had my way, that woman wouldn't be superior here." To which Teresa's God immediately responded, "Teresa, if I had My way, she wouldn't be, either."

This sense of sharing one's beefs with God for the state of His/Her creation was very much part of Teresa's personal friendship with the Divine. In one lovable quote, she took God to task when things were particularly grim, with these words: "No wonder you have so few friends, God, when you treat the few you have so badly!" She applied humor to this old human dilemma, and took the sting out of it. Teresa worked at forgiving God by airing her grievances in a friendly but firm way.

Any way you word it, you have to ask the age-old question of how there can be evil in a world with an all-powerful and all-loving God. In 1984 I faced a triple header: two major traumas at once — my first firing and the death of my mother — and a deeply disillusioning hate campaign in my neighborhood against group homes for young adults with physical and mental disabilities. It was heartbreaking to see so much of human evil and divine tragedy in one year, and I said in bewilderment, "God seems determined to show me every kind of evil in the space of this one year." I felt like a slow learner in a total immersion class being forced to learn a new language, and I didn't like it.

I didn't like it because the lesson I was being immersed in was the heaviest one anyone can be faced with. A few people may never be faced with it. For better or worse, they go through life with the illusion that there is some kind of rough justice in this world, and no gross injustice ever strikes near enough to home to jolt them out of it. But two people helped me in my loss of innocence to understand that when we open ourselves to God, even the triumph of evil in this world can be a step toward transfiguration.

One was the Jewish writer, Elie Wiesel, a child of the Holocaust. Growing up in concentration camps, he spent childhood and adolescence in a living hell, and emerged an adult. In the talk I heard him give at this time, he spoke of rescue coming too late. Someone in the audience asked what he meant, since he emerged alive. I understood exactly what he meant; rescue came too late for children of the Holocaust to save their *joie de vivre*. Life could never be the same, and the child who went in could never fully emerge. How can you ever enjoy anything again in life when you have seen human beings degrading one another in every possible way day after day, year after year? Eli Wiesel's childhood lay buried in that camp. His capacity for egocentric enjoyment of life's pleasures was buried. Never again could he live for the kind of selfish pleasures most of us seek daily.

But looking at his beautiful face, in which wrinkles of suffering and of caring for others were intermingled, I listened to his story about the life he had built, traveling to serve refugees in Cambodia and around the world. The miracle was that a new and better man had emerged. The man who had been resurrected was able to care for others — to give to others joys he could never know for himself in the same way. Through Wiesel's caring, other children would experience the joy of childhood innocence and in that larger joy he could live again.

When we have lost our innocence and learned to live redemptively, we can begin to live in the spirit Christ did, solely for others. We find beyond the loss of innocence that one who loses everything in this life does indeed gain an immortal soul. Recently I came across a book on the spiritual advantages of a painful childhood, and it pointed out the many gains that we can claim from pain, even in childhood. I have always believed that it is a healthy instinct to try to protect young children from pain, because trauma is most likely to be damaging to the very young. I still believe that, but this book reminded me that as we grow up, we can learn to transform even the anguishes we have experienced when we were small, and become more empathetic and larger souls from them.

Children who are suffering need adult support in order to emerge safely from their problems. One study of sexually and physically abused children (among both those who did and did not repeat the pattern on their own children) found that the main characteristic that enabled some to avoid repeating the cycle of abuse was that they could identify *one significant adult* who had understood and validated them in childhood. I have known many adults embittered by pains and abuses, but I have also known others who were in some way picked on as children, yet who managed to use this experience to become sweeter, kinder, more gentle and sensitive people.

There are many different reasons given for the existence of evil. No answer I have ever heard satisfies me completely on an intellectual plane — I have to reach to the spiritual level before I can accept it. But all religions agree that the one thing we can do about evil is to transcend it by our response. Only in this way can God and we triumph together in the face of evil. My mother's life was rooted in the beautiful words of E. Stanley Jones: "to turn irritation into iridescence." I too am a humble learner in that school.

Leslie Weatherhead, the great British theologian, learned one day that his beloved sister had terminal cancer. She was told the same news, separately, and then Leslie went to visit her. Leslie was shaken to the core, but his sister was radiant. She took one look at him and said, "Leslie, what is the matter with you. Don't you know that all those things you've been writing and preaching for years are *really true?*" Then she added these beautiful words, "I am proud to be trusted with cancer."

Dr. Mary Verghese is an Indian woman who overcame all the barriers to education for women of her culture, and went on to become a doctor. A group of new medical graduates went out for a picnic together to celebrate. The driver, showing off and driving recklessly, tried to pass another car on a hill. Mary was thrown out, and became a paraplegic as a result of her injuries. Her dreams were shattered, and she had to go through all the stages of shock, grief, and rebuilding. The driver asked her to sign a petition for clemency for him in court. She met challenge after challenge. Eventually she became a hand surgeon, a specialty she could pursue with her limited bodily resources. But more important, Mary Verghese learned step-by-step to forgive God for this catastrophe and to find the opportunities in the new life she had been forced to explore. God allowed her legs to be taken, but also gave her strength to grow so that she could be a shining example for all of us in transcending handicaps. Her moving story is told in a book called *Take My Hands*.

There is an amazing group of people in the USA who call themselves Murder Victims' Families for Reconciliation. Every one of them is a living miracle of forgiveness, for they have confronted the ultimate horror of having a loved one murdered, and have learned to forgive through God's grace. In the power of turning their lives so fully over to God's power of forgiveness, every one of their lives and faces shines for all of us. Their annual report features a page on each one, half of which is a picture, and the rest of which contains a brief summary of their experience and a short paragraph of their core philosophy about it.

Every one of those faces shines so brightly that I can just look at them for spiritual refreshment. But I will just mention one here. Sunny Jacobs sits in an upright yoga position with a shining smile of peace on her face, her hands before her in a prayer position. She spent seventeen years on death row in Florida, toward the end of which her husband was executed. Two years later, before they had managed to execute Sunny, the innocence of both was proven beyond a doubt. Her husband had been murdered by a vengeful judicial system, and she had spent seventeen years of horror on death row, all for crimes they did not commit. I cannot comprehend how she could have forgiven all this, let alone how her body and face can shine with positive energy and peace. But she has, and she has clearly forgiven God. Her own short statement says it all:

Life has given me many challenges, which I choose to take as opportunities... I learned this on Death Row. I chose life, health, forgiveness, and love... I have dedicated myself to an end to violence — in all its forms... This is the way I must give back to the universe. Love is the answer. Fear is the enemy. We must choose the world we want and work toward making it happen every day in our own lives.

So, in the loss of innocence is our greatest opportunity. Sunny Jacobs, Elie Wiesel, and others have learned to forgive God, and have been transformed by their loss of innocence and their gift of grace. When we too have forgiven God for our loss of innocence, we can turn to the ultimate challenge, the forgiving of those who have hurt us.

Forgiving Others

Forgiving others is an even more misty challenge, and I can only offer some pointers along the road. My first breakthrough came about thirty years ago, when I was experiencing the discovery of my adult faith, following the death of my sister's little girl. Each day was a wonder of spiritual joy as I discovered age-old truths, which were new to me. I wrote to the minister of the church where I grew up, offering to share with this beloved congregation in a Sunday sermon my discovery of adult faith, and my gratitude to them for having provided the foundation for it.

The minister who received this letter was relatively new. He may have been unaware that I had preached from the pulpit before, and he had not experienced the decades of service to the church of my mother and siblings and I. He wrote me back a letter that was narrow and hostile, in which he went out of his way to attack Quakerism, calling our founder crazy, and saying a number of other unpleasant things. He closed by saying that he certainly was not going to turn *his* pulpit over to somebody like me!

I was of course stunned and angered, and my spiritual peace was blasted. I went through days of wrestling for forgiveness for that man. I kept trying to forgive him by understanding him. I would justify his position, going over the reasons why he might have felt that way. But because I was convinced he was wrong — I still am! — I would then respond in my heart with all the reasons he could not be justified, and a battle royal would rage inside me till I was angrier than ever.

Finally, one day I managed in my prayer battles to be truly still. It was one of only a handful of times in my life when I have heard an almost audible voice in prayer. The voice was in my heart, but it was so clear, I remember to this day the exact words: "You don't love him because HE deserves it. You love him because YOU deserve it."

With that revelation, I gave up the struggle to understand him, and let myself love him because I deserved that peace of soul. I quit trying to justify him, or like him, or agree with him in any way. I simply loved him because God made me for loving, and I didn't deserve to be turned aside from that divine purpose by a man as small as he seemed to be. I never forgot that lesson, although, as with most great lessons, I have had to apply it again and again in new situations.

A profound friend gave me a second piece of the forgiveness puzzle. She reminded me that few of the greatest human beings in the history of mankind have ever been understood or appreciated in their own time. Why should I expect anything different? My first lesson was that I deserved to love; my second was that I should not expect very often to be understood fully by others.

Diane Kennedy Pike has a profound saying which is a mystery to me, and which I have put into my own slightly different words: "Have no expectations, but only divine expectancy." My children challenged me once on this, arguing with some truth that human relations and friendships are virtually impossible without some expectations of fair play and treatment in return for the trust we give. Yet, that saying contains the kernel of a great truth, and it is in expecting other people to behave as we think they should that we most often fall into the great traps of self-righteousness and even of hate.

Having expectations of people leads us into the pit of score-keeping on others, and leaves us wrestling all too often with self-righteous, unforgiving anger. My husband frequently reminds me that what another person says or does has a lot more to do with what is going on inside them than with the essence of who I am. Understanding this truth frees me to accept them for who they are, and I don't even have to wrestle with anger and forgiveness: the battles they are waging with themselves are essentially their problem, and only when they intrude deeply into my life do I need to get involved. We are often reminded that everyone is entitled to their own feelings, and this is true, but we have the ability and the responsibility to manage what we do about those feelings. Some people are much more easily angered than others. Correcting our thinking can save us a lot of wasted energy on anger we never need to experience. It takes practice, and it doesn't help to be angry with ourselves when we forget, but lowering our expectations of others and remembering not to make their problems ours can free us up enormously. It did for me with that minister.

When we expect to be appreciated, a great lump of indignation grows within us, resentment builds, and forgiveness comes hard. Get over the idea that you or I will be fully or frequently understood in this world, in our lifetimes. Was Socrates? Was Jesus? Were any of the saints? As my friend said, "It is a luxury for anyone to be understood in this lifetime. Don't expect it to happen very often."

Yet I still wrestled bitterly for a long time with how to forgive the board of my Bail-Out Program in 1983. They would not even acknowledge that they needed my forgiveness. How do you forgive those who *acknowledge no wrong?* They seemed to have ground my most generous gestures callously under their feet. The night they had a closed meeting in my office to discuss me, with no one to represent me, I had left them flowers as a goodwill gesture, in spite of my deep hurt. Even our clients had someone to represent them in court, and they were charged with real crimes! Yet their response to my flowers had been to keep me in agonized suspense for five days after the meeting, telling me nothing about the results till I finally, furiously, demanded them.

So I felt torn between my Christian desire to make forgiving gestures, and my sense that, based on their responses thus far, these people would probably abuse such gestures. They might even misread them as an acknowledgment on my part that their many cruelties were justified: what a galling thought that was. I was torn for weeks by this dilemma.

Then I achieved a tentative truce within myself. I realized that regardless of this board's inability to receive my gestures in the right spirit, for my own peace and growth, I had to forgive. I harked back to Harold Loukes' great quote, which had become a bulwark of my life: "An act of love that fails is just as much a part of the divine process as an act of love that succeeds, for love is measured by its own fullness, not by its reception." This was a new expression in my life of the early truth that I had to love others because I needed to love, not because of their deserts, or of their potential or likely response. But I was still baffled as to how it could be expressed, for while I was not totally responsible for their response, surely it was a part of love to reach out in such a way as to increase their potential capacity to grow, too.

When I had given up hoping to understand any more than this groping feeling of blind faith, I received an answer most unexpectedly. The answer was as familiar in words to most readers of this book as it was to me, yet it was as if I had never heard them before. They spoke to me with all the force of a fresh, blinding revelation, when I least expected it.

I was talking with a beautiful man whose life is a shining example of Christian dedication, Maurice McCrackin. I was nurtured in childhood by my mother's reading of Mac's adventures about going to prison and being thrown out of his pulpit for his conscientious refusals to pay war taxes. When I met him and he became my friend during my loss of innocence, his coming into my life seemed a very precious gift. Mac is a man of very strong principles, but utterly lacking in bitterness toward those who have tormented him with their smallness. As he spoke with me, he quoted, in relation to some of his experiences, the words of Jesus, "Father, forgive them, *for they know not what they do.*" Bells began ringing in my head, and I didn't hear another word he said for several moments. Hearing those familiar words from a man I had revered from childhood, at a time when I was wrestling with all my heart and soul to find forgiveness, it was as if I truly heard their meaning for the first time.

Here was a direct answer for me! Suddenly, God had given me understanding of something I had thought I would never understand. It was precisely because my board might *never understand what they were doing*, in the spiritual sense, that I had to forgive them. I was not responsible for their response. Moreover, I was not responsible that they knew not what they had done. I was *only* responsible for forgiving them, for my own sake, for God's sake, in that same spirit to which Christ on the cross has called us all.

Once I understood that it was my part to forgive them, and that I was no longer responsible to be their disciplinarian or to force spiritual enlightenment on them, I began to find peace toward those who had hurt me most. But there were always moments when something would arouse the old hurts, and bitterness and anger would well up within me. Did this mean I had not really forgiven?

I came to the conclusion that it did not at all. When someone has inflicted irredeemable wrong on you and those dear to you, and shows no inclination to redeem even what little he or she can, you would be less than human if you didn't feel some anger toward their actions. I do not believe Christ calls us to pretend such anger doesn't exist, or to believe that it is wrong. Is it wrong to feel outrage toward someone who raped and killed your child? Not at all. Moreover, we are responsible for our will, to keep it turned toward forgiveness, and for our actions, which must be bent on goodwill and kindness. Our emotions, the bridge between those two, are not always going to follow immediately the direction of that will. We need to respect their right to be felt, but to keep the will and the direction of our lives focussed on forgiveness, without feeling guilt when our emotions still respond with outrage to some fresh salt in a bleeding wound.

But I believe it would be wrong to surrender oneself to that outrage, by directing bitter vengeance toward that person. It is wrong to want destruction and evil to fall on them. Love means wanting what is truly best for the other person. Spiritual growth is painful for those who do wrong because it involves recognizing their wrong actions. So loving one's enemies is willing what is best for them: their ultimate enlightenment. That wish is both healthy and natural. Heaven and Hell are closely akin: in both we are able to feel the real effects of all the good and bad we have done in this world, as they are experienced by those we have lived among.

I pray for those twin gifts to fall on my opponents, my allies, and myself, the just and the unjust alike.

But there will always be moments when you feel again that primitive, narrow hurt. Don't be angry with yourself for that. Accept the anger as part of you, and then turn it to that love which is willing what is best for the other: ultimate growth and the facing of responsibility. The difference between a Christian and non-Christian approach is that the latter may consider revenge as a long-term goal. I freely acknowledge my anger — without guilt for feeling it — but I will not consider vengeance and hatred. It should be noted, of course, that Christians do not have a monopoly on morality. No major world religion — Islam, Judaism, Hinduism, Sikhism, or any other — condones vengeance, despite the actions of extremists who claim divine purpose. All espouse the basic principle of the Golden Rule: "Do unto others as you would have them do unto you."

Visualization is a tool that many have found helpful in working things through. Wilma Dirksen, whose daughter Candace was murdered, herself once explored revenge through visualization. Plagued with such bitter anger and pain, she finally let herself imagine what she would like to do to the unknown person who wantonly murdered her beloved daughter. She decided death was the only answer, and she mentally lined him up against a wall. Then she checked her inner sense, and her anger still mounted. It was not enough for one child murderer to die for Candace's death: ten should pay the price! So she lined up ten child murderers against that wall, and watched them machine-gunned to death. To her surprise, she felt no satisfaction. As each one fell, mortally wounded, she heard the wailing of the parents and others to whom he was beloved. Then she realized that she could not wish to bring to anyone else the bitterness that had come to her. That visualization made real for Wilma her firm commitment to find a better way.

Bill Pelke, whose grandmother was murdered, tells a similar story. Bill's grandmother was a saintly woman who taught Sunday school all her life and loved kids. Ironically, she was murdered by a gang of teenage girls for the small amount of cash in her home. At first, Bill joined his family in wishing for the death penalty for those girls. Then, when one of them, fifteen-year-old Paula, was sentenced to death, something in him drew back.

He was in court when he heard the sentence read and then heard Paula's grandmother break into a despairing wail. He saw in his mind's eye his own grandmother weeping too, as Paula's grandmother was weeping. Suddenly Bill knew with perfect clarity that this was not his grandmother's way, or her wish; she would not have wanted this response to her tragic death.

Bill went on to make something remarkable and positive come out of his grandmother's death. He became the leading advocate for commuting Paula's death sentence. He corresponded with her, he reached out to her family, and he traveled, speaking about this call. After the girl's sentence was commuted, Bill Pelke became a founder of Journey of Hope, a group that brings together families of murder victims who oppose the death penalty. Bill's simple, pure Christian faith radiates whenever he speaks. His grandmother's death has passed on to him the beauty that was hers.

Most of us are not as far along the spiritual road to forgiveness as Bill Pelke or Wilma Dirksen. But we can choose their path, and tread it no matter what events God sends us. We can commit ourselves to the *process* of forgiveness, even if it takes us many years to forgive. Great wrongs that are never redressed may take a lifetime in that process. Again and again I have found that events will revive the original emotions of a great hurt, and that I will have to live through some of the anger and rededicate myself to the forgiveness. Each time I have to find the best way to express the spirit of forgiveness in a new situation. Nor is every step I take monumental or wholehearted.

Recently, a woman in a workshop I was facilitating told of a somewhat stilted letter she wrote to the boy who had beat up her daughter. She concluded, "It wasn't a really selfless letting go in love, or a big gesture, but it was all I could manage." I assured her that it *was* a big gesture, and it was indeed selfless. When we are on the road to forgiveness the path is hard, our steps may be faltering, but we are unquestionably moving in the right direction. For me, it is a glorious challenge, not a burden. To be called to forgiveness is to be called to the highest challenge in Christian living.

When we pursue that calling wholeheartedly, we are given gifts along the way. I received one such gift nearly a year after my board fired me. I was singing a beloved hymn, "Face to Face," with my daughter. We were harmonizing happily, and its words of promise about the beauty of the life to come reached me deeply. Suddenly, I found myself spiritually carried into the next life. I saw and felt the hugs and greetings and joy we will find. And to my amazement, I found myself in a cluster with those very board members! The scene was like the ending of a play when all the characters that have been slaying one another pop up and take their bows, holding hands and smiling at each other.

In that spirit, my board members and I smiled sheepishly at each other, as we looked back over the whole silly production, murmuring, "Well, we got through it pretty well, didn't we? But we could have done better." There was a peace, a beauty, and a sense of perspective in that ultimate reconciliation which took the sting and self-righteousness out of it. I believe that when we are on that arduous but wonderful path, God gives us glimpses like this to help us along. For I have never doubted that God is with us all the way, cheering us on in the great challenge of forgiving one another.

Risking Trust and Love Again

> Most people here [concentration camp] are much worse off than they need be, because they write off their longing for friends and family as so many losses in their lives, when they should count the fact that their heart is able to long so hard and to love so much among their greatest blessings.
>
> — ETTY HILLESUM, An Interrupted Life

Daring to risk love again when we have been deeply wounded by bereavement or betrayal or abandonment is no easier a lesson than forgiveness, yet we will deal with it at much less length. One thing I said repeatedly in my first loss of innocence is, "I am determined to learn the right lessons, not the wrong ones." It is so easy to learn the hardening ones, "I will never trust again," or, "I will never really care about anyone/anything/any job/any relationship again." Such a reaction, however horrendous our loss, is like trying to kill a fly with a nuclear bomb. We blast all our future hopes of growing, loving, caring, involving ourselves in everything that matters in life, and like sulky children resolve not to eat our porridge if we can't have our desert when we want it. We are just too frightened to come to the table again and would prefer to starve ourselves.

As with all the steps we have talked about, the key is to take one tiny step at a time. It would be abnormal and foolish to emerge straight from deep grief into a whirlwind of activity. But we can begin to reach out in small, tentative, often difficult steps to those most likely to facilitate our further healing.

At first we long only for the loved one we have lost, the home that has burned down, the health that is gone, the relationship that has been betrayed. But if in the midst of that acknowledged longing we can reach out to someone who needs us, who welcomes our part in his or her life, it is a positive first gesture toward the risks of loving. Yes, we will be hurt again. Yes, we must learn what we can to avoid needlessly repeating destructive and painful patterns. But abandoning the risks of loving is like giving up the glue that holds the whole world together. We can't live as whole beings without risking love and trusting again. So we learn not to trust con men with our savings. We learn how to care better for our health. We learn so many other things, and we use that learning to build new relationships, new hopes, new dreams, and new experiences that link us to all that is best in life.

Accepting Failure

To all those who have written terrible books on how to be a success, I dedicate this terrible book on how it's perfectly all right to be incompetent for hours on end, because I am, and so is everyone I know.

— STEPHEN PILE, dedication, Book of Heroic Failures

A third thread in rebuilding is accepting failure as a healthy, valuable part of life. Jean Vanier refers to his beloved people with mental disabilities as criminals in our world, because it is a crime in our society not to excel. Too often we regard failure as a crime. One of my earlier disillusionments came when a man we had loved deeply, whose cause we had defended publicly, left us stranded with a large loan we had co-signed for him. We were hurt financially and personally, but we were also publicly embarrassed, after we had stood strong for months for his innocence and virtue. In trying to cope with my feelings, I unearthed a wonderful novel, called *The Sinner of Saint Ambrose*. In it the author makes an obvious analogy between the Roman world and ours. Near the end the hero sums up many of the author's views:

Our whole age, our whole Roman world, had gone dead in its heart because it feared tragedy, took flight from suffering, and abhorred failure. In fear of tragedy, we worshipped power. In fear of suffering, we worshipped security. In fear of failure, we worshipped success.

Yea, in fear of the intensity of life that is in tragedy, we worshipped the coldness of death that is in power. In dread of the fertile growth that there is in suffering, we worshipped the sterile obediences of security. In terror of the healing love there is in failure, we worshipped the corrupt denial of one another that there is in success.

During the rising splendor of our 1000 prosperous years we had grown cruel, practical, and sterile. We did win the whole world. We did lose our own souls... But outflowing love, and the joy of vital integrity, and the creative in-dwelling of God returns to the soul when the acceptances of tragedy and suffering and failure liberate a man from the sterile grasp of all his fears...

I had nearly memorized that passage in my early twenties, and so it was with me to look up and make mine on a deeper level when I most needed it. The creative acceptance of tragedy, suffering, and failure are a great deal of what this book is about, and what my life is all about. I have said for years that the peculiar challenge I have been given in this life is how to fail gloriously and graciously. But indeed I wonder if it is not a challenge that all of us are given. For without being willing to risk failure, we cannot tackle any tasks worthy of our mettle. Limiting ourselves to safe, easy tasks limits our world to tight, boring, fenced-in circles, far too small for the challenges we are capable of taking on.

One year, our neighborhood decided to work together on a multicultural fair to express the strength of our crowded, sometimes defamed, but wonderful multicultural Jane-Finch community. A group of us who shared the vision gathered, but the more we got into it, the more frightening it became. There were so many details to cover: insurance, tents, toilets, health department, permits, policing, outreach, publicity, fundraising, planning... Every meeting became more challenging till some of us panicked, and began saying, "I don't think we should go ahead with this. I've never done anything that was not a success, and I wouldn't want my name to be associated with this, because it is too risky and difficult." Some of those people withdrew, and the ones who continued to come fretted so that it was harder for the rest of us. But most of us felt it was worth trying, and that *to fail at something worthwhile was better than not to try at all.*

In the end we brought off our multicultural fair, risking not only bad organization, short funding, and conflict, but risking the whole event on good weather. Miraculously, it came off, as many risks I have taken have; but many have been creative failures too, and those are just as important to my life as the successes. I found these views expressed very well in a book on anorexia by Cherry Boone O'Neill, *Starving for Attention.* In it, Dr Raymond Vath writes:

> The idea that people cannot tolerate disapproval was challenged, as was the belief that life above reproach is an attainable goal.
>
> We challenged these unhealthy premises with four concepts that seem to be helpful. The first is that if an activity is worth doing, it is worth doing poorly, because, second, practice will make better but not perfect. Third, it is better to try and fail than to fail by not trying. Fourth we should fail at about half the things we do in life so we can discover our limits.

I liked the challenge of the last — we should fail about half the time if we are functioning on a creative level in life. I was very pleased at a recent workshop when someone said in the closing evaluation, "What I liked best is that you know how to say, 'We blew it, so what did we learn from this, and now let's get on with it.'" That attitude has been one of my goals in life, so it was heartening to see that it was coming through. I have always said as a supervisor or person in authority, "I am never interested in blaming or punishing. I am interested in figuring out what went wrong, so we can learn from it." Why shouldn't we accord ourselves that same constructive attitude?

If you think about it, you will remember that some of the most obnoxious people we know are too perfect. A few flaws and failures make us more acceptable to our fellow human beings, who also fail, as Pike says so pithily. Join the human club, get your feet wet with failure. You'll find the water's a bit chilly, but once you get used to it, the swimming is invigorating!

So in reentering life, keep on the path of forgiveness, and dare to risk trusting, loving, and failure once again. With those guides, the new directions will be rich with all the pain and learning you have gained from the trauma you have experienced. You can bring to it a deeper sensitivity to all those around you who are suffering. You will find that includes virtually everyone. Most wonderful of all, you know now experientially that, come what may, you have the tools to grow creatively through it.

Supporting Loved Ones in Building Anew

> 'Tis not enough to help the feeble up,
> But to support him after.
>
> — SHAKESPEARE, *Timon of Athens*

Everything that has been written in the preceding sections should help you help your loved ones deal with the giant challenges of forgiveness and risking anew. Beyond that, this stage is probably the easiest of the three for you and for them. Precisely, it is because you expect it to be easy; however, it is natural to become impatient. There will still be ghosts that pop up to pull the griever back to his or her grief, and they will need your patient listening at such times. The gift of not saying "I'm tired of all this!" at such times makes you a rare friend indeed. You need the fine art of being crystal clear about the wrongs they have been given to deal with, without encouraging them to cling to them. Help them take their own steps along the path of healing to the point where they are ready to let go of the grievances, but don't tell them they are unimportant now because of the passage of time. They have to find for themselves that new priorities have emerged, and your recognition that the old wrongs were and are real will help that process.

You need to learn to rejoice with them, having mourned with them. Don't keep looking for new crevices — allow the two of you to enjoy the good in the new directions together. It is a rare friend who can do both, but you can expand your skills in sharing joy as well as sorrow. This is the time when there should be rich gifts to share in both directions.

Finally, a friend to someone in the reintegration stage needs to be very flexible. The griever may have a new job, spouse, home, and these things may change her or his ability to phone you, meet with you, commune in the ways you used to. Don't feel abandoned. Accept it as a probable outcome of the changes in his or her life. If you value the relationship, offer new ways of getting together, and also accept it if the demands of learning new skills or forming new relationships just means there is less time for you. After all you have given, this may seem like a betrayal.

One friend of mine who was incredibly loyal and helpful when I was ill was quite hurt that, when I entered a new, highly demanding job, I did not have the time for daily phone chats and weekly long visits. I felt guilty, for I sensed her feeling of desertion, but short of giving up the job, there was little I could do about it. We did talk about it, which was the best treatment, and we came to a better understanding. Try not to take personally changes that are not personal, but talk out the feelings that arise from such shifts. Now is the time to share more of your own feelings with your friend. This will help to reestablish a balance where you share listening and support more equally once your friend's time of extreme neediness is over.

Even if you do all this, it is possible that you will have an even harder gift to give. You may have to let go of the relationship. Whether because the person is moving to another locale far away, or because life is taking them in new directions which carry them away from you, sometimes the new integration and healing of a friend leaves you behind. It is difficult to know when this is genuinely the case, and when we let things come between us needlessly. But if the cues are clear, your greatest gift to your friend is sometimes to let go. If, for instance, your friend's new and healthy relationship requires directions that are counter to yours, it may be the right course just to let go. The greater numbers of partings in modern life are definitely sad and often make us feel fragmented. One of the good things to learn is how to part in such a way that we can take up the relationship again should our paths come closer. Meanwhile, there are many ways to maintain a friendship at a lower level.

Life is a moving train. I am a very loyal person, and I want relationships to be lifelong. But we can't stop the train to stay in the station with current friends when life changes and growings are carrying us both to new locales. We do not abandon one another, but we do learn to let go positively, to say goodbye, cherishing the good memories, and hope that our paths will cross again at some future date. But if they don't, we can still carry the treasures of that relationship in our hearts, and appreciate the person we have become. Whatever your friend's new direction, you can take pride in having weathered this storm with him or her. If you have lovingly shared the initial waves of shock, borne together the seemingly endless dark period of grief, turned the corner of acceptance, and learned to respond to the changing needs of the rebuilding stage, you are a rare friend indeed. Moreover, your learning will aid you when your own journey comes through the dark tunnel of one of life's traumas.

CHAPTER 9

The Journey Continues:
Faith, Hope, and Courage

If you chain me to this sickbed for the days that I have
  yet to live,
They would be too short to thank You for the days that
  I have lived.
If these pages be the last that I ever write,
May they be a hymn to Your goodness!
— FREDERICK OZANAM, founder of
St. Vincent de Paul Society

O ZANAM WAS NOT JUST FOUNDER of St. Vincent de Paul and a
saint in his commitment to God's beloved poor. He was also a brilliant theologian, whose writings did much to keep Catholicism alive in his time. He was only forty when he entered his final illness, with a young family to support, and in the midst of major writings he needed to finish. If anyone had reason to call God on a bad deal, Ozanam did. Yet those words of praise were among the last he ever wrote, and he never stopped singing God's praises.

It is hard for us to realize that such faithfulness is not an automatic gift to a few saints, but a hard path which they struggle along just as we do; the only difference among us is the strength and duration of our commitment to that path. I was trying to walk that path as summer merged into fall. We had a lovely six week visit from Corinne and our two grandchildren. We got to see Pippa's emergence from a few frightened steps to long toddles around the house, and we got to hear Owen's imaginative four-year-old play and conversation. We explored every local playground, and each day was an unfolding wonder.

The physical demands of two young children distracted us so much that it was not until they had gone back that I realized fully how much the combination of prayer, chemotherapy, and natural supports had helped. On September 1, I went off all painkillers, and had no further need of them. The fall opened out as a period when I was restored almost to my full energy and health, despite some side effects from the continuing chemotherapy. We cherished every power regained, and I especially cherished normal digestion again.

One of the tricky things about my situation was that no one knew how long it might go on. Even the pessimistic doctors admitted that I could live two to three years. This was tricky for all of us, and meant, of course, that the one greeting over-and-out kind of response, which is normal in this busy world, where we are not very conditioned to dealing with ongoing challenges in the lives of our friends, didn't fit at all. Ongoing caring gestures are things anyone can do, like giving flowers given long after the initial burst of sympathy has passed. That ongoing support was there for me. Many of my friends continued to write, call, and tell me in person of their faithful prayers for my health and strength.

It takes a kind of courage to look death in the face, but I found myself strengthened by two things, in addition to my deep faith in immortality and my support community. First, I have a vivid awareness now that we are *all* dying all the time — it is just that some of us are more aware of death and nearer to it than others. Second, there is the old story of the woman in labor, yelling, "I've changed my mind — I don't want to go through this thing!" It is easier to be courageous about hard steps where we know we have no choice, than those where we have some element of choice still. The gift of life in this world includes the gift of death, and having enjoyed the first, we have to accept the second as part of the whole gift package.

The Supportive Community

Many of the letters from I received from friends talked about faith, hope, and courage in the struggle. Jim Consedine, Catholic worker priest of New Zealand, and ally in our penal abolition struggle, spoke of the Communion of Saints where the living and dead all merge into one family of God. He added, "Whichever side of the curtain we are on, know that your spirit and all you have tried to do over the years will be carried into the work we do in the future. None of the seeds planted will be lost — all will be carried to fruition sometime."

Several people wrote about faith. My niece in Alberta wrote, "I can see clearly how your living faith in God is carrying you through. I know your body is sick, but 'It is well, it is well with your soul.' I can still hear your beautiful voice singing that hymn." My friend Wayne Northey spoke of my ministry in pain to others, and of our need to celebrate each moment, continuing to pray for healing with full faith, and yet accepting the mysterious truth that "Though He slay me, yet will I trust!"

Another group of friends expressed anger and a sense of injustice. A deeply Christian friend of mine delighted me with these words: "I went looking in pharmacies and other stores for an appropriate card. None said *damn* in great, big letters. And none said *we love you and pray for you* in big enough letters. Another dear friend wrote of how my illness resurrected her struggles over whether God was fair. All of us have to wrestle over and over with the eternal question of why God allows bad things to happen to good people. An agnostic friend, so loving and eager to help, summed up a lot in these few powerful words, "You always fought injustice. I know you will fight this." A friend, who admitted she was struggling with the injustice of all this, concluded, "I can pray for you that you remain strong and keep your faith. Emotionally, however, I struggle, but soldier on. The apostle Thomas, although doubting, stayed with the flock."

Many wrote of hope. A prisoner friend prayed that God would give me hope, knowing that hope itself can cure and heal. He added wittily that he felt I already had my spot reserved in heaven, and there was no need to rush to get there. My amazing friend Bette Hilmer had paired with us in the wonderful adventure of enabling a hopelessly institutionalized young man to experience, for the first time, six whole months outside of institutions. She quoted Emily Dickinson, "Hope is the thing with feathers that perches in the soul and sings the tune without the words, and never stops at all." Uju Agomoh, had struggled, with my support, to get to the 8th and 9th International Conferences on Penal Abolition and was organizing the 10th in Nigeria. When I told her I would not be able to come, she wrote back: "Ruth, you will be part of it all — in flesh, body, and spirit. You will be in Nigeria come August 2002. This candle that you have put on will shine in Nigeria come August 2002 and you, Ruth, will pass it to all the participants on the Nigerian soil. Believe it. Wish it, and live it." This was indeed hope made concrete!

A friend who had lost a daughter a year before wrote of the epiphany of her daughter's last months:

> Because of her joyous release in those last months, she has left a house saturated with joy. When I walk about now, and see an expressive picture we took in those months, I am flooded with a sense of peace, happiness, and truly, miracle. This is an experience I could not have conceived of when I was writing of the more common encounters with grief. No one could have explained it to me before I lived through it... Maybe it will help you remember that even when and if that time comes, there can be a glory in it too. You, of course, are not so likely as Barbara was to dance in heaven and spread mischief. You will probably organize the angels!

Her words inspired me with another goal: when my time came, that my passing would be so linked with the divine that my family and friends might experience that same joy which is, as Teilhard de Chardin says, "The most perfect expression of the presence of God."

My friend Jeanette Schmid, who had succeeded me in my paid job when I retired, nominated me for a major restorative justice award (which I received that fall) with words that recognized the transformative aspect of my living through this experience. She concluded:

Her ability to see light where others see only darkness has encouraged so many of us to review our own perspectives on life. Many of us have experienced this again recently. Ruth is dealing with multiple challenges: retirement, the diagnosis of a terminal illness, the impact of chemotherapy, the immediate news that a close relative has passed away. Yet in the midst of this trauma, she is considering the needs of others... beyond herself.

I was reminded of the precious words of Minnie Lou Haskins, "I said to the man who stood at the gate of the year, 'Give me a light, that I may walk safely into the unknown.' And he said to me, 'Put your hand in the hand of God, and that shall be to you better than light, and safer than a known way.'"

Lynn Scott spoke of the oddball curves life tosses us, and prayed that her angels would join mine in lessening pain and lengthening my useful life on this plane. So we each faced the mystery in our own way, but it was important to acknowledge that the mystery was there, and that our finite minds could not penetrate it fully.

Sharing the Journey

My friend Carol Spiegel told me of how Cardinal Berndine's cancer helped him connect with others. Many people expressed gratitude at my own willingness to share this journey. It is their appreciation that makes me willing to offer it to readers here, believing that the more we can share life's deepest journeys, the more we will strengthen one another in the most important challenges of life.

A new friend I had met shortly before he left behind all the comfort of his life in Canada to work on a spiritual project in India, wrote that my sharing of this journey helped him in his own adventurous one. Colleagues of my husband said that my sharing helped them to better understand our needs, and uplifted them in their own struggles. My cousin John wrote, "This is just to tell you that Nancy and I are finding your 'weekly' letters to be very important to us. They keep us feeling as though we are there. And they're exciting and inspirational. Please remember that we're following every event closely." A month later he sent this bulletin, "Nancy and I are reading your messages with awe, admiration, tears, laughter, and inspiration." Bill Phipps, then Moderator of the United Church of Canada, took time out of his exhausting schedule to tell me that the sharing of my journey had inspired him.

Finally, a friend from New Zealand wrote, "I am sitting with tears in my eyes and joy in my heart as I have just completed your inspirational letter. What a gift your honesty and intimacy is. Just as you have transformed so many lives and experiences in the social justice area, so too are you working at an even deeper level of transformation. I am grateful to be able to share some of these moments... Thank you for your courage to make a difference in inner and outer worlds, and to be willing to accept and pass on all the love that surely flows to you."

My friends, family, and acquaintances also joined in cheering our good news in the early fall: my symptoms had disappeared, and the halfway through chemo CT-scan showed a shrinkage of the tumor! My friend Rick Prashaw spoke of my confusing the hell out of people with my rapid recovery, and hoped I would continue to confuse them. He added, "As an educator, you know the value of shedding confusion on certitude." It was indeed confusing to people who had already accepted my inevitable death to see me bouncing around in the fall, almost as present and energetic as ever. But behind all the wonderful support of my friends and family there still lay a frail, sometimes scared, sometimes worried, and confused human being.

I had hoped to spend our first year of retirement quietly, nurturing our spiritual life and our retirement relationship as a couple, and later beginning outside activities again. As it had developed, we had spent the first six months moving "from meetings to medics," spending a lot of time on medical resources for Ray's emphysema and my cancer, but also, perforce, a lot of time learning more about healing prayer and about meditation. As my strength was returning, I was stepping back cautiously into some of my social justice activities.

In late October we decided to treat ourselves to a one-week visit to Salmon Arm, a community of 16,000 where we had bought our retirement home, and to which we had originally planned to move the month before, in September 2000. We wanted to make contacts there, to seek experiences to give us a place and community to look forward to joining, and Ray wanted to reward me by celebrating the halfway point in my chemotherapy. We had a wonderful time, and by one of God's miracles, a major restorative justice award was announced. It came with very little notice, and was to be presented to me in Vancouver that very week! So all we had to do was take our rented car on an extra five hour drive over the beautiful mountains, and celebrate a wonderful evening.

In November, my niece Laurie, whose journey in this life has been so close to mine, sent me the text of her own sharing at the adoption ceremony she had organized in New York City. Laurie has an adopted daughter from China, and has worked hard to enrich understanding of the beauty and challenges of adoption, and the need to recognize both. The ceremony cele-brated all aspects of the adoption experience for those who participated in it. In her speech she shared her gratitude for her childhood with us and then quoted part of the letter I had written in response to Joy's "everything-I-don't-want-not-to-have-said letter," quoted in Chapter Seven:

When I look at you sitting here, I see people who are caretakers of wonder. This means you are giving a child the gift of a sense of won-der so strong that it becomes an antidote against future disappoint-ments, against things that are artificial; and it keeps them believing in the sources of their strength.

If you're lucky, you've met people like this. Maybe it was in the orphanage where you lived, or in a foster home, or maybe you have teachers, relatives, neighbors, babysitters or ministers and rabbis with whom you share your life's mysteries. When I grew up, I had my Aunt Ruth. When I was six, she introduced me to the Land of Oz. When I got older and no one else seemed to understand, she was always there with her open ears and heart.

Just a couple of months ago, she called to say she had cancer — it's the kind the doctors say can't be healed. But I haven't given up on hope, and won't let her stop believing in miracles. Still, you're proba-bly thinking it would be pretty hard to find wonder in this hard news

— you don't know my aunt. I'd like to read what she wrote to her adult daughter. As I do, please think about the caretakers of wonder in your lives — bless them, and smile.

"I am sorry I can no longer protect you from this and other pains. It is hard for me to see Dad crying since the news came. It's also good to hold each other and cry together, and let it out. The risks of loving mean that inevitably we feel pain from seeing each other suffer. Yet as I've said often, the risks of loving are *always* worth taking.

Parents are meant to protect young children from pain as far as possible. But I've seen from watching you and our other children that everyone must learn how to grow *from* suffering. Trying to protect our children from all suffering is to take away life's greatest opportunity. When we can't, we need to accept the mystery that God allows such pain to all of us. Our greatest growth often comes from it. So my prayer is that this experience will help you to grow from the already beautiful person you are into an even wiser, even more empathetic, and even more resilient, faith-filled person. And I think that likely."

Christmas with Cancer

Christmas, a time of wonder that had always been so special to me, was drawing near. In recent years, as my distaste for materialism had deepened, and as our children had grown into full adulthood, we had struggled with how to observe it, but still the magic and wonder persisted. Now I faced a Christmas with possible death from cancer staring me in the face. The unknown, "Will I experience healing, an actual physical miracle, or will I die from this?" went on, day after day. I kept trying to walk that tightrope between absolute faith that God *could* heal and *wanted* to heal, and the mystery that many good and faith-filled people had not been healed.

On December 23rd I had a very upsetting call from my oncologist, who told me that the final CT-scan of the chemotherapy period had shown no improvement (although also no growth) and who also told me of three possible cancer sites. We had thought there was only the one major tumor and were suspicious of an uncertain spot on my spine. When I tried to tell him we had never heard of the new spot in my remaining kidney (which of course would be fatal since we all need at least one kidney!) he ignored this and insisted I must have known.

It was crazy-making to be told that I knew what I didn't know, and the previous day, his nurse had also treated me impersonally in a variety of ways. The call left Ray and me in the first tears we had shed in a long time and feeling that, for the second time that year, the medical profession had given me a clear death sentence.

Doctors seem to have swung the pendulum from one extreme to another. Thirty or forty years ago, a patient could not extract the information that they had cancer, or some other serious condition, for love or money. Lying to the patient was considered essential. Now patients with any kind of negative prognosis are told repeatedly in a variety of ways that their situation is hopeless and they should get on with dying. Is there is no happy medium between these two extremes?

A couple of hours after the doctor's call, my niece Laurie called from New York, and she picked me up emotionally right away. She spoke of hearing the fear back in my voice, and reminded me not to give in to it. She also reminded me, "Doctors don't really know anything. Oh yes, they have a little medical information, but nothing really definitive.... Don't forget all the books and articles we are reading, many of them by healing doctors who do understand the whole person. So don't let yourself be deflated by this little bit of information this doctor has when we have so much more we can understand, seek, and do!"

The exciting books we were reading, by true healers like Dr. Bernard Siegel and Dr. Carl Simonton, opened up a new understanding for me that hope, prayer, nutrition, exercise, meditation, and visualization were all part of the healing treatment for cancer and other diseases. Their approach affirms that we do influence our own bodies, and that patients must be in charge of their own healing. I learned the wonders of our immune systems, which are the only thing that can ultimately heal us. I learned how our thoughts and our stresses can affect those precious immune systems. I began to honor mine as I had never done before, and began to try to become a full partner in my own healing.

Dr. Simonton established his cancer unit with only patients who were declared terminal and hopeless. Even so, in his first group forty percent were alive four years later, and the average life span of all far exceeded the norm, and with a comfort level far superior to others. The very first patient was so satisfied with the experience of curing himself of cancer completely with Simonton's meditation and visualization strategies that he went on to cure himself of arthritis too!

Simonton writes, in *Getting Well Again*:

> We are sometimes asked, "Aren't you giving your patients false hope?" Our answer is "No," we are giving our patients reasonable hope. Our approach does not guarantee recovery. But the question of "false hope" suggests that people should never hope if there is a good chance they will be disappointed. Such a belief provides no basis for living a full life, or for dealing with a threat of life.
>
> We enter marriage with no guarantee that it will be a happy and fulfilling experience. If we approach marriage with the expectation that it is bound to fail, it certainly increases the probability that it will fail. A positive expectancy does not guarantee a successful marriage, but it increases the likelihood of a good marriage, and improves the quality of the relationship.

Dr. Bernie Siegel points out that about seventy percent of patients tend to do whatever their doctors tell them is going to happen — recover or die — which is a frightening responsibility. I suspect many oncologists are dealing badly with unresolved grief from their inability to save the lives of many of the seriously ill patients who come to them. It is vital that they not visit their problem on their new patients. Siegel says that the fifteen percent of patients he describes as "exceptional" are considered ornery by their doctors, but are also acknowledged to get well far more than average patients do. They take charge of their own healing, they make demands on their doctors, and they chart their own course – not irrespective of medical wisdom, but after hearing it and taking it all into account. There is much wisdom beyond medical wisdom, and we need to balance it all in this struggle of the human spirit for healing.

Bernie Siegel's and Carl Simonton's meditation and visualization tapes are truly heavenly, and their words embrace the whole of life: their own medical expertise, but also all the emotional and spiritual components of healing and wholeness. Carl Simonton's voice sounds amazingly like Mr. Rogers' voice from the old children's TV shows. And why not? Both of them manage to convey, in their voices and in their work, a love for the whole of unseen humanity. Both Siegel and Simonton were decades ahead of their time and very much criticized by their profession for recognizing the patients' vital role in healing, for including spirituality and emotion, and for giving hope where other doctors gave only despair. Now the world is catching up with them, and their work is best-selling.

Another remarkable book is *Cancer: 50 Essential Things To Do*, by Greg Anderson. The author was told he had a month to live, refused to accept that, cured himself by a challenging and balanced approach, and has been completely well for fifteen years. In that time he has interviewed and surveyed 15,000 survivors of "terminal" illness. His book is about the common elements in these survivors' stories. He says they balance eight essential strategies, and identifies the last as key to it all, integrating all the rest. They are:

- medical treatment
- positive beliefs and attitudes
- exercise
- a sense of purpose in life, balanced by play
- social and community support
- improved diet and nutrition
- creative thinking
- deepened spirituality

In his introduction to the Anderson book, Simonton says:

For over twenty-five years I have been working with an approach to cancer that includes the physical, mental, and spiritual... Many of you who read this book are undoubtedly in a very difficult situation. Do not despair. Keep your hope alive... Live this moment. Forgive, love. You'll then know the power of hope... and you will be on the path to getting well again.

All of these great healers speak again and again of the need to hope. Anderson writes of those who have criticized them for giving "false hope": "I believe there is no such thing as false hope, there is only reasonable hope, a medicine worthy of consumption in large doses." He then speaks of doctors' negative predictions as "false hopelessness... Healers instill hope. They do not schedule death."

It was with my oncologist's negative words ringing in my head that I sat down to write a long letter to friends and relatives. One of the wonders of e-mail is the speed with which communication can happen. Within two hours of sending off my e-mail letter of December 23rd, we had received four of the most wonderful letters I have ever had. Interestingly enough they came from two Christians, a Jew, and a Muslim. I will share here just a few words from my Muslim friend, a former employee of mine who had just been through the intensive prayer experience of the Islamic Holy Week for Ramadan. She concluded with some beautiful verses from the Qur'an about the birth of Jesus, and then added these words:

From the Night of Power to the Miracle of Christmas, all these verses are sent your way, dear Ruth, just to affirm our belief in God — God only. Men (even those endowed with medical degrees) cannot and should not give verdicts about human life. Only our God (of all believers, whether they are Jews, Christians, Muslims, or of other faith) who is the Most Gracious and the Most Merciful, knows what the future holds for us, irrespective of whether we have or we do not have tumors for doctors to detect, to treat, and to follow up with competence, care, and compassion. Ultimate cure comes from God, and all we've got to do is trust in God and keep on praying and praying and praying, as we do in your case because *we love you*, and many of us owe so much to you. And we are a big number! Please enjoy the present moment, and have a wonderful Christmas with your family. Much love from our house to yours, Erin.

The letter I had written also evoked a remarkable rage in my correspondents, even though I myself was only mildly angry. I was more disheartened than angry. Given that some of my rants about workplace problems had not evoked even a fraction of that anger, when I had been so very upset, I almost wished I could figure out the formula for bringing out so much anger in others! I reasoned that a part of my friends' anger originated from beefs they had with their own doctors, and that my experience was a catalyst, calling up all that anger from many sources. In addition, maybe the very fact that I had understated my own beef, and mentioned repeatedly my understanding of why the doctor and nurse had behaved as they did, was more effectively provoking than when I overstated the sins of the opposition. As I expressed my frustration with the negativism of my oncologist, friend after friend expressed their understanding of how limited doctors were: "The final answers are not in their hands."

My former boss spoke feelingly of her own recovery from cancer, her deeper gratitude for each day's gift of life, and reminded me of healing scriptures like Jeremiah 30:17: "For I will restore health to you and heal you of your wounds." My special new friend Bill Pelke, a leader in the group Murder Victims' Families for Reconciliation, whose life motto is "The answer is love and compassion for all humanity," was transformed by his successful struggle to forgive his grandmother's young killer. Bill wrote, "I continue to lift up your health to our Father, the great physician. You are in His hands, as we all are. They are loving, nurturing hands, and I know He loves you very much. I know He will never leave or forsake you."

My niece Amy, who worked in a hospital, mentioned how regularly she saw that optimistic patients with positive attitudes were those who healed. A friend from India gave me a beautiful exercise to practice: "Envision yourself surrounded by Divine Light from the soles of your feet to the top of your head, and that this Divine Light is completely healing you. Do this as often as possible. I wish you wellness! "

I found the anger of my friends validating, healing, and also a little amusing. It roused me from the unhealthy state of discouragement to the healthier one of realizing it was more of an occasion for sharing anger, and for continued action. I set a new long-term social action project for myself and my friends: to do something about the deplorable state of doctors' education that seemed to leave so many of them utterly inept at dealing with the emotional and spiritual needs of their patients.

My dear friend Matthew spoke of the need to dream large enough in this struggle:

Tackling the impossible is something you always have been about. For people like me, you have opened the space to say, "Let's not just look at one little symptom, let's call into question the whole rotten system." When you looked at prison abolition, people must have sat back and said, "Nah, that's too big to confront," yet it is now part of daily parlance in the field. And though there must have been indescribable moments of doubt in your mind this summer... there was part of you which set the wheels in motion and concluded: this too shall be transformed from something that most people (especially doctors) feel is impossible into something which can be dealt with and reduced and eliminated. Anything that confronts you is in for a tough, non-traditional battle because you choose to "fight" through transformation rather than violence. So it is that the karma you have put out has come back to you in many multiples.

Many spoke of their lack of surprise that, with my strong spirit, I was recovering so well. This was good and it was heartening, but it begged the question, "If I get worse again, is it then my fault for not trying hard enough? Will I have let down all these wonderful friends?"

Still another friend spoke of believing that we choose when we pass over, and concluded, "My wish for you is that you feel complete with this life and ready to move on, and that you do it as peacefully and painlessly as possible. Of course I really wish that you not leave quite yet, but that is your decision, and I will support you either way you choose."

Here was one of the mysteries — if I could only be sure that I could choose! The uncertainty of my situation yawned before me; some felt my will and spirit had a lot of choice, others that I had very little. The feeling of powerlessness is part of the burden of cancer, which sometimes seems to be gnawing away at us in spite of our will and spirit to live. The oncologist told me in so many ways that it was my fate, my destiny, and almost my duty to die. Yet the healing doctors and cancer writers I most respected offered reasonable hope to all, and emphasized that our wills and spirits did have a huge effect both on our getting cancer and recovering from it. Where was truth in all this?

My last meeting with the oncologist produced the information that quite possibly there was no cancer in my remaining kidney at all — it could just as well be a small enlargement, a common enough normal condition. I wrote a courteous letter to my oncologist thanking him for the good he had done but requesting that my last Toronto appointment be with someone willing to consider the possibility that I could be one of the thousands of people each year who recover from seemingly terminal conditions.

In our family we had a wonderful Christmas Eve song, celebrating all the anticipation and magic of Christmas Eve. We sang it over and over all day December 24th, and each happy note resonated with the joy that was there and the joy that was to come. But on this December 24th, I got caught in a negative mantra. I found myself thinking, on the heels of that terrible news, "This could be my last Christmas on this earth in this lifetime." I thought that again and again until I remembered that this was not a constructive mantra to be repeating to myself, and I resolved to focus instead on our future plans and on the fun we would be having together as a family. It was another reminder that we can change our thinking, for I let go of that doleful thought, and focussed instead on the present joy.

It was a lovely Christmas. Three of our four children were with us for the 24th and 25th, and two were able to stay well beyond that. We played family games, we followed the dear old rituals, we had the usual slow distribution of gifts, we sang Christmas music, and we had a bang-up, unashamedly generous Christmas dinner. It was possible to celebrate in the midst of this challenge. I received a beautifully handmade shawl from a friend in New England that I had met only once in my life, years before, though our mail relationship had continued in an occasional way for years. The shawl was accompanied by these words: "Shawls, made for centuries, are universal and embracing. They enfold, comfort, mother, hug, shelter, and beautify. They are symbolic of inclusive and unconditional loving. You, of all people, should receive a shawl." Its soft warmth, along with the hours of labor in making it, was love made manifest, and reminded me again of the true spirit of Christmas, so much deeper than the bows and wrappings.

Surrender

I said earlier that I would speak a little before I close this story about why my friends in this cancer struggle have been so much more sensitive, supportive and present than I found them in my earlier research and experience with traumas. I can think of three possible explanations. First, we are experiencing something of a spiritual revival, as our world economy falls apart in this era of rule by multinational corporations. Perhaps this renewed spirituality provides a sounder base for supporting one another. The second possibility is that I have led my friends through such an arduous chase through my checkered career of risk-taking that the set who have survived all this, or even joined up in the course of it, are an unusually hardy lot. It is also possible that my own experience with trauma, as both sufferer and supporter, has enabled me to learn more by now about how to ask for and affirm support, and that too may be a factor. I am inclined to think there is some merit in all these arguments, but am fully satisfied with none, and invite readers to think it out for themselves.

I cannot conclude this story without a word about my husband, Ray. All our children have been very supportive. Joy even got a special phone deal that enabled her to make long calls to us nearly every evening – once again love made manifest. But Ray has been his usual indescribably loving, caring, generous self in so many ways I cannot even begin to detail them, from transporting me everywhere and being with me in every chemotherapy to talking things out in the night and taking over more of the housework. Most of all is the tenderness in every word and every deed. If cancer is an opportunity to enrich marriage, Ray has seized our opportunity and made it a golden one, for both of us.

This is a continuing story, with no immediate ending. In a sense, every day has its own outcome. One of the keys the many guides who have helped people through this difficult terrain agree on is that we have to go on planning. So we are going ahead with our big move west, away from a community where we have thirty years of roots to one where we will be building new lives in our retirement. I am currently planning to visit a friend in Alberta who has been praying for me in long distance calls every two weeks, and who wants to gather all her prayer resources in an intensive series of prayer healing sessions. She lives in Lethbridge, where our daughter Joy is, so I look forward to all aspects of the visit. Thirdly, I am going ahead with plans made long ago to organize a major family reunion of my mother's extended family in our new town of Salmon Arm, next July. We will be celebrating one aunt's 89th birthday and our 40th wedding anniversary.

For life is something to celebrate, and to adventure in together. Cancer has taught me many things. I have learned a lot about healing prayer, but even more about the power of community. It is our community of loving pray-ers that has kept me alive this year, and which has inspired me day after day. It has been hard choosing all these warm words about myself from the letters that have come in, but the lesson here is that community is about affirming one another. Cancer has been a bridging experience for me, and a growing experience for me, Ray, and our communities. I have learned again that, as Shakespeare said, "There are more things in heaven and earth than are dreamt of in your philosophy..." I have learned to value the very process of uncertainty. It is hard not knowing what the future holds, and finding the yo-yo cycle pushing me up and down at times.

Sometimes I wake up, with the shock of it hitting me again, and I feel fear. I ask myself: What am I afraid of? I don't believe I am afraid of either death or dying in any great measure, although of course the unknown aspects of each are a little scary. So I have concluded that I am afraid of making the wrong choices in the struggle to find the right path to extend my life here. There is so much advice, there are so many resources, and so much of it is conflicting. It is an awful responsibility. But then I realize that all I can do is follow the best advice I can get from my own God-guided common sense, from my friends, and from the books and sources that seem wisest – from both medical and holistic sources. When I have done all that, I must do the best I can to follow through. One of my mother's favorite Bible verses applies, "And having done all, to stand."

Striving always for that balance between resilient hope and acceptance of the seriousness of the challenge, I found once again the usefulness of that concept of "surrender" to God. In my youth I had thought surrender weak and cowardly, an unworthy thing for God to ask of His/Her created beings. I preferred the idea of commitment, which encompassed the passion and courage that were so harmonious with my personality. But over the years I had come to understand that surrender was a very useful concept too. There is in each of us a capacity for both good and evil. The ability to exterminate our fellows, to torture, to hate, is in us all, as is the ability to be a Gandhi, a Mother Teresa, or a Martin Luther King. It is that self-will that each of us has which has to be surrendered to the higher needs of love and inclusion. Giving up our selfishness is anything but cowardly or annihilating. For when we surrender our self-will, a whole world of adventures in the risk of loving opens out before us.

So I came again to face surrender here. It was not giving up the struggle to live, but something much bigger and braver. Although many prayer teachers tell us we should believe completely that we are being healed, others talk of surrendering a beloved baby into God's care, trusting that whatever God allows will be blessed, and that healing often comes precisely from such total surrender. I think I am working toward that with my own life on this earth. It is a paradox, but I believe completely that God wants my physical healing, that God has the power to make that happen, and that prayers can assist in that process. I also believe we cannot understand the mystery of why healing comes to some and not to others, despite their great faith, great value, and strong motivation to live.

Jean Patterson, a Costa Rican Quaker friend, reminded me that all my dear ones were fighting my ill health, by my side. She also quoted the words of Peace Pilgrim: "An obedient attitude toward God will bring you into constant awareness of God's presence, and then fear is gone. When you know that you are only wearing the body, which can be destroyed, that you are the reality which activates the body and cannot be destroyed, how can you be afraid?"

Another friend, whose schizophrenic son had committed suicide, had spent years on the journey of grief. She spoke of the therapy of surrender: "When we pray with heartfelt sincerity, 'Lord, take all that I have and all that I am,' our darkness lifts, and we walk in the Light again."

So in surrendering my life on this planet to the Creator who gave it to me, I was not abandoning my faith in my own healing. I was merely deepening my commitment of my life back to God, and recognizing that God can do good things from any outcome. In order to trust God, we do not need to understand the mystery of how so much goodness and power can allow so much evil, pain, and tragedy to continue. In trusting to both the goodness and power of God I put myself and all those working on this cause in touch with the greatest power of all, the power that comes with total surrender of our lives to God. I also feel more at peace. I have not given up expectation of cure, but I have given up the feeling that I have to pit all my energy against the power of cancer, and pull my life along by my own bootstraps, as it were.

So I work at surrender to God, at being guided to make the right choices, and at valuing the very process of meeting cancer eye-to-eye each day. And having done all this, I stand before God, ready to cherish each moment of this life. It is indeed true that, as one friend wrote recently, "The doctors have only a small part of truth, and you have resources that could make the doctor's head spin." The greatest resource of all is learning to float in the waters of faith, so that I can trust God fully with the life God alone has given me.

One friend wrote that "death is a clarification on both sides of it — it compels us to go wider and deeper than the material ego on this side, and it makes every moment here infinitely precious. On the other side, it brings others to full appreciation and clarity of what you have been and are... You will be more a presence with the life you have led after your bodily instrument rejoins the all than you are now." He added that his intuition was that this was not my time, and that these intuitions were generally borne out.

Whether I find complete physical healing and a much longer life here or whether I graduate soon to the next spiritual plane, I know now that cancer too is a part of God's world, and an opportunity to learn how to walk through shock, grief, and rebuilding. Walking boldly through it to the music of the magic flute, I have found that cancer is difficult, frightening, and often upsetting; but ultimately, it holds no terrors as long as we continue to tune in to that divine music.

We have no choice but to walk forward with faith and hope, love and forgiveness for all humanity. This is the path of healing for all the world, healthy for everyone, and realistic in the largest sense of the word. So we pray that every one of you can walk, as we have done, as far as you can on your own faith journey, "putting your hands in the hand of God, which shall be to you better than light and safer than a known way." Like all challenges, there are times when we wish we did not have to embrace it, but whenever we have done so with our whole hearts, we have felt the sparkling joy of discovering new adventures in the risks of faith and love.

CHAPTER 10

Gifts of the Darkness

> For everything you have missed, you have gained
> something else.
>
> — EMERSON

WHEN I TOLD SOMEONE I WAS writing a book on transcending trauma, and that the last chapter would be on the gifts of trauma, she said, "I can't wait to read your book, and I'm going to skip to the last chapter first. I need the hope that there is something positive coming out of all this misery." We all need that hope, and the good news is, there is hope. Most of us wouldn't have chosen this path to those gains, but the human animal is intractable at times, and we must ask ourselves whether we have sufficient empathy with others in pain to make these gains without experiencing trauma and pain ourselves. You may discover other gifts of trauma, but I am very conscious of four, and will share with you something about each of these:

- deepened empathy
- true security
- becoming more nearly the person we can become
- being transformed by the power of enduring the unendurable

The Gift of Deepened Empathy

God needed a back like our backs on which to receive blows,
and thereby to perform compassion as well as to preach it.
— MEISTER ECKHART

When I lost my job in 1983 a dear friend said to me, "Your firing was like your graduation. All the love and work you put into creating and running that agency were like your courses and exams, but your firing was your graduation." Strangely enough, I liked what he said. It was novel, and it gave me a new perspective.

One of the things that haunted me that first summer of my loss of innocence was the vicious cruelty of a new member of the board. He didn't even know me, but on the night of my final firing turned on me and said, "Why don't you just get out? You're a disgraced, discredited employee of no credibility and no worth. Why don't you just go right now?" Although shock and grace combined to enable me to handle that situation amazingly well at the time, it haunted me that summer, and affected my sleep. I would lie awake, tossing and turning, and asking myself, "How could *anyone* treat a person in such an awful situation so brutally, let alone someone on a human services board?"

I thought of confronting him in some way, and I thought sometimes of more positive gestures to exorcise this ghost. I had a lot of trouble accepting this reality: that the crowning tribute of my board to me, their only acknowledgment of nearly four years of dedicated, quality service in founding and running the organization was to call not only my service, but me, utterly worthless!

The beautiful words of Jean Vanier had been so much a part of me that they were almost my very life's breath:

The miserable can do without a look that judges and criticizes,
He needs a comforting presence,
    That brings peace, hope and life,
And that says:
"You are *you*,

168

Someone mysterious, infinitely precious,
What you have to say is important,
For it comes from a human being
   In whom are some seeds of the Infinite,
Seeds of love and of beauty
   Which must germinate in the soil of your misery
In order for humanity to fulfill itself."

Of course, I knew I had often failed to live up to my ideals. God knows also how earnestly I have tried to see through the eyes of Christ the beautiful spirit in every person the world has labeled worthless. I tried to see it in this man who said these harsh words to me. It seemed ironic that I should now be labeled worthless, especially in front of a group who had for years experienced the best loving service I was capable of giving. When the best that is in you is thrown back in your face as worthless by those who are apparently in the best position to judge, it is hard not to find it disturbing.

One of the good things it did for me in those wee hours, when I wasn't just stewing in my own anger and hurt, was to make me re-examine the life experiences of the people we call "our clients," the fodder of the justice system, those who give us employment. I thought of their lives, and compared them with mine. I had had every blessing most of them had never enjoyed, and yet, how often they showed loyalty, graciousness, compassion, good-will, and courage, beyond what I was achieving now.

In my forty-nine years of life up until this point, I had just this once encountered a crushing experience, been dragged in the mud, and finally called worthless as I was cast out. In less than half that number of years, most of them had rarely or never experienced the kind of love and loyalty that had been my daily nourishment. I had been a beloved fourth child with parents who cherished me. My older siblings protected me, and my main responsibilities as a child had been playing and growing. In school I had been the delight of my teachers, and when I grew up I did indeed make a nearly perfect marriage. My whole life till now had been one long walk in the sun.

In contrast, our "clients" had been labeled school problems, delinquents, scapegraces from multi-problem families, crazies, unemployables, prisoners, alcoholics, addicts, and criminals. In other words, worthless. This happened not just once, but every time they encountered an authority figure. Badly clothed by middle-class standards, they had little idea how to fit into a typical classroom. Many had undiagnosed learning problems and went through the living hell, year after year, of trying to function in school without being able to read properly! Every task was an exercise in futility and, to top it off, no matter how good their efforts were, they were castigated for "not trying." No wonder they began acting out early, in self-defense, trying to protect their tattered self-images from the further degradation of trying once more and failing.

I went over my haunting questions again, and found that even we "bleeding-heart social workers" write off clients who "aren't motivated" with a callousness that exceeds the brutality I was so upset over. I was surrounded by loving family, supportive friends – even strangers who sympathized with what had happened to me – and I was upset because a few people, one in particular, had called me worthless. Prisoners are surrounded *all their lives* by people who treat them as worthless.

I was appalled at their hitting me when I was so very vulnerable. Yet, when a person encounters our justice system, they are attacked first by the police, then often by whatever family or friends they may have. They are subjected to the brutal labeling experiences of arrest, and spend weeks of torment awaiting trial, sometimes even in jail, increasingly treated as cattle to be processed. At what ought to be their breaking point, they undergo the ultimate horror of a court trial in which every aspect of their lives is publicly jeered at and displayed in the worst possible light.

Then the judge's role is to berate them further, and announce the supposed beginning of their punishment! After that, for the unlucky ones who don't get a discharge, the "real" punishment is supposed to begin — all the degradation that goes with imprisonment. No wonder someone in a "justice agency" thought it was fair game to kick me when I was already down. His verbal assault was mild compared to the "normal" treatment our clients received at the hands of the "justice" system.

When we speak of a person as "salvageable," it implies that they are currently trash. I saw with fresh eyes that our clients have the label "worthless" dunned into them every day, all day long. And we wonderful, compassionate, helping people, if we reach out to them for a few weeks or months or years, resent it if they fail to grasp successfully our one helping hand amid a thousand pushing them down into the quicksand.

Yet here was I, a strong, resourceful, self-confident person with deep faith and many loyal friends, deeply upset because one voice out of many meaningful others had denounced me as worthless. A new awareness dawned on me, and I gained a total respect for the courage of prisoners and other "worthless ones" in life, and I was awed at the courage they show.

So how did that help me — what was the gift of this trauma? It didn't make what he had said any better. But it did begin to put it into perspective. I began to see that there was a gift to be grateful for even in this. I remembered my friend's comment about it being my graduation ceremony, and I began to think of that terrible speech as the conferring of a new degree: my diploma as a Worthless Person. Like most of the fortunate of this world, I had been born a Valued Person, and carried my VP degree with me into the world till now. But the gift of this experience was that I had earned my WP degree! Some people are born WPs and almost never know the possibility of being treated as anything but worthless. Others, like myself, have to achieve some great heresy or failure in order to make it. But I began to see that beneath all the pain of this particular degree was great value.

The great Japanese Christian Toyohiko Kagawa had written these inspiring words:

God dwells among the lowliest of men. He sits on the dust-heap among the prison convicts. With the juvenile delinquents, He stands at the door, begging bread. He throngs with the beggars at the place of alms. He is among the sick. He stands in line with the unemployed...

What I began to understand in a flash of vision was that it was not enough to stand *with* the convicts, the beggars, and the unemployed. It was necessary to *be one of them*. The great gift I was being offered was the awesome opportunity to know directly, from personal experience, a tiny portion of their daily, yearly, lifelong lot. It was a life-changing experience! All I had gone through — the humiliation, the loss of status, the pain of seeing those I loved hurt, the separation from the work and people I loved, and the destruction of the values I cherished in the agency I had founded — all this was crowned by this characterization of myself as worthless. But as I began to exorcise this ghost, I discovered that to *become* one of the worthless ones was the only way to dedicate myself totally to my belief that no one should ever be treated as worthless.

Gandhi said: "I do not want to be reborn, but if I am reborn, I want to come back as one of the untouchables." Every truly great spiritual leader has caught that vision in his or her life. And here I was being given it, gratis! Far from resenting it, I should have been grateful at having achieved this honor: to be recognized along with the humblest derelicts who sleep on our streets, the most forsaken of God's children in the hostels and institutions and dark corners of the city.

One of the most exciting gifts of this trauma was the awareness that I was no longer just one of the great, overly-washed middle-class world I inhabited, but that I was also part of that other world. I know now that I have a foot in both worlds, and that I straddle both. This is the first gift of the darkness of trauma: we gain empathy we can gain in no other way, for we experience for ourselves the deep suffering in this world. As Jean Vanier puts it:

The question is not, Why does God permit them to suffer?
But, Why does God permit the rich not to share?...
The tragedy is that people have a heart, and don't love.
The greatest affliction is to reject someone,
Because it is an affliction of the heart.

By working with the world's worthless ones and understanding their suffering, we can build a world where every human being is always treated as beautiful and beloved in the sight of God. So the first gift of trauma is the gift of true empathy, a vibrant empathy that comes only from resonating with the same pain that vibrates all around us. Until we have been there too, we are deaf to the tones of that pain. When we open ourselves to the growth that can come from trauma, we open ourselves to the divine gift of empathy.

The Gift of True Security

> That a man has a restful and peaceful life in God is good. That
> a man endures a painful life in patience, that is better; but that a
> man has his rest in the midst of a painful life, that is best of all.
> — MEISTER ECKHART, on "True Victory"

Wilberforce, that incredible man who ended the slave trade in the British
Empire, fought against dueling, child labor, and so many other evils, and
was a rich man most of his life. But in his later years, his son went bank-
rupt, and Wilberforce insisted on giving up his whole fortune to his son's
creditors. This amazing man then said, "I know not why my life is spared
so long unless it be to show that a man can be as happy without a fortune
as with one."

This visionary statement has inspired me in my traumas to say to myself,
"I don't know why my life has been spared this long, unless it is to show
that a person can be just as rich without a career and worldly recognition as
with them." In that strength is ultimate security. Bars and locks and bank
accounts and suburban ghettoes cannot protect us from the inevitable risks
of this world. But ultimate security is ours when we know that, with God's
help, we can cope with absolutely anything! It is heady stuff indeed.

The New Testament says it powerfully in Romans 8: 38-39: "For I am
sure that neither death, nor life, nor angels, nor principalities, nor things
present, nor things to come, nor powers, nor height, nor depth, nor anything else in all creation, will be able to separate us from the love of God in
Christ Jesus our Lord." In this same spirit, there is an enormous power in
accepting the truth that life is sometimes unfair to every one of us, and that,
with God's grace, we can deal with our own injustices, with God's grace.
Getting through life without experiencing injustice is like taking a course at
school without ever having to submit a paper or take a test: it may be easy,
but we don't learn much.

In the same spirit, I have often said that we have given our children deep
security by opening up our home to the world and its woes, for they have
seen that no one is outside the field of our love, and therefore they cannot
fall outside of it. Too often, we make the mistake of seeking security

through exclusivity. Inclusiveness is a much healthier, more reliable form of security. Some years ago, Corinne gave me a beautiful gift of reassurance about this through a dream she had one night. In her dream, the phone rang, and I answered it. She could hear both ends of the conversation. A strange, ugly, threatening voice on the other end said, "If you and your family don't move out of this neighborhood, we're going to blow up your house, and your whole family with it."

In Corinne's dream, I replied with complete aplomb, "You might think that a threat like that would intimidate a family, but if you think that, you are very much mistaken, because we're not frightened a bit!" After that lively exchange, the dream continued. Having shown by this opening that Corinne had complete faith in my ability to deal with any situation, she now showed the same faith in herself. For next the doorbell rang and she answered it. She faced our would-be kidnappers, and she tried to talk them into coming in and having a party with us! But although she could not completely divert them, she talked them instead into taking us to their place and having a party together there. In her dream, Corinne lived the power of turning irritation into iridescence. Her dream demonstrated her faith and showed that she and I could deal with anything life had to offer, using the power of the spirit of love.

That dream told me that I had played some part in helping her find true security in life. Walls and towers are always subject to moth and dust, to thieves and breakdowns, but spiritual security is ultimate security. The only ultimate security is to have faced our worst fears, to have walked through them, to have suffered from them, and to have found that God's way cannot be stopped by catastrophe, hatred, or violence.

So when we can include the reality of trauma, failure, death, injury, illness, and every other kind of calamity in our circle of acceptance – when we no longer deny and hide from them – we find true security. These too are part of God's world, and only in learning to accept and live with them can we find that depth of security. The mystery of true security lies in going through trauma with our eyes and hearts open. Then we can accept all the terrors of shock and the pain of grief, and in them find the fertile roots of vibrant new growth.

The only security we can give each other is to know we will never be left alone in our grief, that we are *not to blame* for tragedy, should it befall us, and that we are not crazy to feel the passionate waves of grief that bring us to healing and growth through tragedy.

The Gift of Becoming

I said to the man who stood at the gate of the year
"Give me a light that I may tread safely into the unknown."

And he replied, "Go out into the darkness, and put your hand
　　into the hand of God
That shall be to you better than light and safer than a known
　　way!"

So I went forth, and finding the Hand of God
Trod gladly into the night
He led me towards the hills
And the breaking of day in the lone east.

So heart be still!
What need our human life to know
If God hath comprehension?

In all the dizzy strife of things
Both high and low,
God hideth His intention.

God knows.
His will is best.
The stretch of years
Which wind ahead, so dim
To our imperfect vision,
Are clear to God.

Our fears are premature:
In Him all time hath full provision.
Then rest: until
God moves to lift the veil
From our unpatient eyes,
When, as the sweeter features
Of Life's stern face we hail,
Fair beyond all surmise
God's thoughts around His creatures
Our mind shall fill.

— MINNIE LOUISE HASKINS

That beautiful poem was a favouite of King George VI of Britain and his wife Elizabeth. King George had never expected to assume the throne, as he was second in line, behind his elder brother Edward. But when Edward abdicated, in favor of life with his beloved Wallace Simpson, the painfully shy George had to step into the breach. Adding to his shyness was a stammer that was only overcome through speech therapy. Just a few years after George became King, World War II broke out. In his Christmas broadcast of 1939, the King read Haskins' poem to his listeners and he said: "A new year is at hand. We cannot tell what it will bring. If it brings peace, how thankful we shall all be. If it brings us continued struggle we shall remain undaunted."

One of the great mysteries of life, and one very relevant to the topic of this book, is why tragedy ennobles some people, as it did King George, and seems to destroy or warp others. We all know people whose deep sensitivity seems to arise from having suffered. This is the gift of empathy we spoke of earlier in this section. But we also know how the cycle of violence or pain repeats itself in many lives. Drinking parents beget alcoholic children; abusive fathers beget abusive sons, and so on. How then can the same input – pain – beget such opposite responses?

This is a momentous question, and I lack the audacity to say I have found the whole answer. But not long ago, I gained an insight, managing to glimpse an important part of the picture. I believe that people who are destroyed by trauma are generally focussed on what they *had* (or should have had) and *lost*. Those who grow from it are focussed on what they *are* and what they *can become*.

Life is like a soap bubble: when we try to clutch it to us, it bursts in our hands, leaving us tearful children with only a sloppy blotch and a memory of joy. But if we take from the bubble its colorful reflective vision of who we can become, then its fragility does not destroy us when it passes the way of all soap bubbles. One of the greatest gifts of trauma is to learn more about the person we can become, and to get closer to being that person. If that is what it is all about, then we don't need to rage at the person who took away our child, our limbs, our job, our house; or at God for taking away our health, our spouse, or our marriage. Instead we find, in each of these terribly difficult challenges, the opportunity to become something more than the person we were. In the same spirit, when we engage in heroic acts of loving and forgiving those who are hardest to love and forgive, we don't usually transform the target of our love as much as we might hope, but the one person we surely change is ourself. When we can demonstrate the courage to go on and build anew, we are becoming the person we are meant to be.

One of our children struggled through a period of self-image problems, as most of us do. We found a wonderful book for him, a children's book so simple and so eloquent, whose message has become a major theme of my life. Its title is *Just One More Block*. It's about a little boy who keeps building block towers, but just as they get high enough to enjoy, he tries to add one more block, and they topple over. That, or his little sister comes along and knocks his tower over.

Each time, he goes through a similar set of questions:

What shall I do?
Shall I cry, shall I scream?
Shall I run to Mother?
Shall I kick little sister?

Each time, he comes to the same triumphant, life-affirming, courageous conclusion:

No, I will build again, for I *am a builder*.

That little boy's challenge has become the challenge of my life, and it is the challenge of life to all of us. When life has knocked over our blocks, what do we do? Do we cry, do we scream, do we run to mother? Yes, we do some or all the above, and all of them help us cope with our shock, grief, and rebuilding. But in the end we have to face the ultimate challenge: are we going to build again, and recognize that we are builders, or are we going to cave in to disaster?

The greatest gift of trauma is the discovery that we are builders – builders who have the courage to build again and again. It is heartbreaking work sometimes, but each time we build anew, we can almost feel our spirits expanding, for God made us to grow, and trauma is one of the great fertilizers of the spirit. The gifts of trauma are not easy to take, but all the great spirits have accepted them gracefully, and in so doing, have cast light upon our path. The path of trauma is a dark journey through shock, grief, and rebuilding, but that path leads us towards becoming a person more wonderful than we had dreamed possible.

The Gift of Transformation

> I'm done with great things and big things, great institutions and success, and I'm for those tiny invisible molecular forces that work from individual to individual, creeping through the crannies of the world like so many rootlets, or like the capillary oozing of water; yet which, if you give them time, will rend the hardest monuments of human pride.
>
> — WILLIAM JAMES

Many years ago in Washington, D.C., when I was a young housewife with preschool children, Joe Rauh taught me one of life's great lessons. Washington, D.C. was governed by a very racist group of southern Senators because an old law, based on the assumption that Washington would consist entirely of civil servants who should not vote for the government they served, took away self-government and gave it to Congress. The law had been maintained as Washington became the first majority black city in the USA, and the power was used very abusively. The fight for self-government in Washington was not just a fight for democracy; it was a fight for justice against the most blatant racism.

President Lyndon Johnson, a great president on racial issues, used all of his extensive political savvy, and all of his political influence, as the drama unfolded. Joe Rauh, a longtime liberal community leader and lawyer, had been leading the fight in the community for twenty years. The two were a powerful combination, but the opposition was powerful too, and they did their best to hold the bill up in Committee. I was tied to my home by my children, and all I did to support it was watch the struggle each day with open mouth over my ironing board. But my prayers, my wishes, and my soul were with it, and I watched these two prime actors with the deepest admiration.

Congress was about to adjourn, and if the Bill was not extracted from Committee in time for passage, it would be dead for years to come, for who knew when there might again be a president and Congress as likely to pass this bill as this combination were? Each hour the thing seesawed, looking like one side or the other had finally won. Johnson called two of his Texas congressional friends back from constituencies to sign the bill out of Committee, and it looked like the bill's supporters had finally won.

Next day the devastating news came. Senator Byrd, a crafty and experienced southern Senator with decades of experience in procedures, had used an unanticipated parliamentary maneuver to consign the bill to oblivion! It had been defeated. I had done nothing on the front lines, but I was so devastated I could hardly stand to watch the news. Just in case there was still some vestige of hope, I turned it on, and learned they were going to interview Joe Rauh. I knew that he knew that bill would have no chance for years to come, and that mattered enormously. We both knew it would cause human suffering and permit the abuse of power, further corrupting the souls of the powerful by enabling then to abuse the rights of blacks and other families in Washington.

So I expected Joe Rauh to look that night like a man should who had just been horribly defeated after a 20-year critical struggle. There was no quick fix for this continued suffering. But when I saw Joe Rauh, I received one of the biggest and most important surprises of my life: Joe Rauh was not annihilated — he was radiant! I still remember almost his exact words. "Don't let our opponents imagine they have defeated us, for our cause is the future. They have won a skirmish, but the future is ours, for justice is ours." Joe's radiance that day taught me one of the biggest lessons of my life, and is a part of the power I have found in suffering. I learned that the truth that we cannot be defeated when we will not.

How disheartening to opponents to see us empowered by suffering and defeat! When we are determined to be too dumb to know when we are beaten, and when we find strength in defeat, then we cannot be finally beaten. In God's time, God's way will triumph, and what matters is that the whole weight of our lives is for that cause. Elijah said it ringingly, "Choose you this day whom you will serve. As for me and my house, we will serve the Lord!" Much more recently someone declared, "You may say that all the efforts of my life for justice are futile, and you may be right. But I beg to declare on which side of the great scales of right and wrong, my life will fall."

When we tune in to that ultimate truth, we touch a power that transforms us. The darkness of trauma passes, but what we learn in that darkness, we possess forever. We gain the power to greet each unjust person and situation as an opportunity: an opportunity for greatness of spirit. Not that we would choose it, ever, but having it thrust upon us, we learn that by accepting it as if we had chosen it, we turn the power of the wrong we are enduring into a transforming energy in our lives and in the world. In recent years many people have referred to a spiritual power they see shining through my life, despite all my manifold weaknesses. I know that what they see is something I have gained by accepting the traumas described in this book.

Thornton Wilder's The Eighth Day is a profound novel about a man wrongfully convicted of a murder, and what happens to him and all his family as a result of these events. The convicted hero escapes "justice" but is an exile, and in his wanderings, he meets a woman who explains the gifts of trauma to him. Her words say much about the meaning behind our journey together through the long, hard, but growing stages of trauma:

When God loves a creature, He wants the creature to know the highest happiness and the deepest misery — then he can die. He wants him to know all that being alive can bring. That is His best gift.

For when we grasp the angel hand that brings us trauma, we allow these challenges to turn the superficial soap operas of our lives into great Shakespearean drama. Tragedy is an opportunity to stretch our spiritual muscles, but an even bigger opportunity to allow God to transform us. The mystery is that our greatest hope in life is to be allowed to face our own Gethsemanes! When we can remember in the depths of a trauma that it is not what we have lost, but what we have remaining that counts, and even more, who we are becoming, then we are being transformed. Pinocchio was transformed from a puppet into a real little boy by learning to practice unselfish love, and we too can be transformed into something much more wonderful.

Bill Pelke is a living witness to personal transformation. He is still a frail human being with faults, but the thrust of his life is one of transformation from tragedy. Bill has for years been a leader in the struggle against capital punishment and a pioneer for compassion and forgiveness. He is a steelworker who heard God's great call to forgiveness after his grandmother's murderer, and who has lived that call day after day. He is a founder of the Journey of Hope, which brings together murder victims who speak out for compassion and against revenge. He lives and breathes his oft-repeated, simple motto: "The answer is love and compassion for all humanity."

Bill has also been very involved in my own work for transformative justice, which I have undertaken through the non-profit group that Ray and I founded, Rittenhouse: A New Vision, and through the International Conference for Penal Abolition (ICOPA), which meets every two years. Transformative justice simply means making healing, and not revenge, the basic goal of the criminal justice system. In his powerful plenary address at ICOPA IX, Bill startled me by addressing one comment to me personally. Looking at me in the audience, he said, "Ruth, you have given me, finally, the word for my experience. I *have been transformed*."

Embracing trauma and transcending it may not be the only way through it, for millions of us have responded to trauma in other ways, but it is the only path that leads to growth. Since there is no way to avoid the traumas of this world, we can choose to embrace them with hope, courage, faith, humor, and above all, love. Bill's life – like those of so many of the others quoted in these pages — gives us the vision and the hope of what each of us can become — transformed.

A Day's March Nearer Home

Being blind and deaf to the material world has helped me develop an awareness to the invisible, spiritual world. I know my friends not by their physical appearance, but by their spirit. Consequently, death does not separate me from my loved ones. At any moment I can bring them around me to cheer my loneliness. Therefore, to me there is no such thing as death in the sense that life has ceased.

Those with sight so often put their entire trust in what they see. They believe that only material things are real. Their sense of the unseen is undeveloped, whereas the inner or mystic sense gives me vision of the unseen.

— HELEN KELLER

I HAVE BEEN STRUCK BY THE BURDEN of living in a faithless society, which persists in ignoring all the evidence from so many sources of the immortality of the human soul and the deep reality of God all around us and in our very beings throughout our lives. A recent study out of California, for example, confounded the medical community by proving that prayer has a positive effect on patients, even over great distance, even those who do not know they are being prayed for.

It is a great mystery why some prayers for healing or safety have miraculous physical results, and others don't. I've never figured it out, and I don't think anyone else has either. The great thing is that, like Saint Paul, I can say it is joy if I continue life here, and joy if I go on. I believe there is much good I can do still in this world, and much I can still learn here, and I believe that is worth the prayers of all of us. Clarence Jordan, in his wonderful *Cottonpatch Version of Paul's Epistles,* puts Paul's words thus:

Whether I live or die, so long as there's a breath left in my body... I will exalt Christ. For it is Christ if I live, and gain if I die. If I keep living, there must be something worthwhile for me to do. I just don't know which I'd rather do, because I am drawn by the prospects of both. I have a deep desire to set sail and be with Christ, for this is better by far. Yet for your sakes it is more urgent for me to stay on here . . .

It is a pity some fundamentalists limit themselves to material over 2000 years old, which contradicts itself over and over. I cannot believe in a God who wants us to remain in ignorance when assurance is all around us if we just open our hearts to it. Nor can I believe that all significant spiritual witness ends with the last entry in the Bible. For contemporary witnesses, start with the many books about near death experiences, and go on from there. Several sources have mentioned that virtually all bereaved persons experience some awareness of the loved one's presence in the first weeks after their passing. Why are we so determined to ignore these messages of love from the people we love?

However, I also find there are people of living contemporary faith who are true companions in my present journey, and I thank God for them, and feel the need to keep close to them. It is hard to accept that this body which — for all my taking it for granted and taking advantage of it in some ways (while respecting it in others) — has served me so well, is deteriorating, and I can do nothing much for it now. But then I realized that *all* our bodies are gradually wearing out, just like old machinery, and it is up to us to develop our spirits, and accept the fact that we are always moving toward that separation, when our spirits will move on to another mode of life. Our bodies are like launching pads given to us to prepare our spirits for the next stage in the great journey of spiritual pilgrimage, and we should no more cling to them than a rocket should cling to its launching pad.

We live in an age that has blindfolded itself to the spiritual realities all around us, with its false worship of science, wealth, worldly power, materialism, and technology. This crisis in my life is yet another opportunity to remove the blindfolds and engage the world at the spiritual level, which is always all around us, and is open to each of us. Even if I do pass on relatively soon, I have been given a greater awareness of the precious nature of every moment in this life. I pray that you too can share in some part of this gift, one of the many gifts of suffering from which we too often turn away in blind grief, instead of clasping the "angel hand that brings it."

I keep thinking of one of the duets Mom played, which Dad and I used to sing, "Forever with the Lord." These lines keep running through my head:

> And nightly pitch, my moving tent,
> A day's march nearer home —
> And nightly pitch, my moving tent,
> A day's march nearer home!

The music is triumphant and joyous, as it should be. We are all each day a day's march nearer home; it's just that I am nearer and more aware of that nearness than I was, and in many ways that is a good thing.

Ruth's Farewell Letter

Winter is on my head, but eternal spring is in my heart. The nearer I approach the end, the plainer I hear around me the immortal symphonies of the world to come. For half a century I have been writing my thoughts in prose and verse; but I feel that I have not said one-thousandth part of what is in me. When I have gone down to the grave I shall have ended my day's work; but another day will begin the next morning. Life closes in the twilight, but opens with the dawn.

— VICTOR HUGO

I have had from my twenties total faith in immortality, and will be sending you all messages to that effect, so listen in when I have passed over. Please pray for Ray and me to deal with this in a way which will help each of you face the challenges that come to you; ways that will inspire others in their faith journey to travel through this world on a deeper level of spirituality. Each of you receiving this letter has added something to the wonderful mosaic of life I have shared. I am tremendously grateful for the sixty-six wonderful years I have had. I have had so many privileges, such a wonderful family, such an incredible marriage, and so many opportunities to use the talents and opportunities God gave me to build a world with more compassion and true justice. I had looked forward to a new chapter in Salmon Arm with our retirements, but it appears the many people who laughed at the idea of my retiring were right in a way they had not guessed, and that retirement in this world is not to be.

I am sure that in the next life I will be given tasks that will be a joy, to build on the cosmic struggle of humanity here. So if I do pass on to the next realm of spiritual activity, I will still be working with you for social justice and building bridges with passion, humor, creativity, and love.

Life is often about letting go of the preconceived plans we had, and accepting the things that happen. I find that, so far, not that hard to do in this instance, precisely because I have already had opportunities to do most of the things I had dreamed of — spiritual growing, marriage, family, friendships, writing, speaking, and making whatever contributions I could to a more just and compassionate world. I have done what I could, imperfectly often, and now it is time to pass these challenges and opportunities on to you.

My love and prayers are with each of you as you go forward in the spiritual and social challenges of today's world.

Twenty Questions for Further Thought

1. What kinds of trauma have I experienced?
2. How have I coped with them?
3. Have I accepted their naturalness and the need to work through them over time?
4. How does it help to see trauma as four stages?
5. How can I tell when I am dealing with shock?
6. How can I tell when I am dealing with grief?
7. How can I tell when I am dealing with acceptance?
8. How can I tell when I am dealing with healing and reintegration?
9. What are some creative ways to reach out to those in trauma?
10. What are some ways of reaching out that I have seen used positively among my friends?
11. Do I remember to reach out to people in trauma?
12. Who do I know now who is experiencing trauma?
13. What do I need to understand in order to help them further?
14. How can we help in a situation where a whole family or group is suffering from a major trauma?
15. Have I ever seen or experienced victim-blaming?
16. Why does victim-blaming happen, and how can we help people to avoid it?
17. Are there people I need to forgive in order to move on with my life?
18. Do I blame God for my traumas?
19. What gifts were there in the traumas I have experienced?
20. Have I looked for the gifts of trauma and nurtured them?

Sources

Alkali Lake Indian Band, "The Honour of All" [video], Williams Lake, 1986.

Anderson, Greg, Cancer: 50 Essential Things to Do, New York: Plume, 1999.

Axling, William, Kagawa, Rev. ed., New York: Harper & Row, 1946.

Beisser, Arnold R., Flying Without Wings, New York: Doubleday, 1989.

Bonisteel, Roy, In Search of Man Alive, Toronto: Totem Books, 1981.

Burroughs, John, "Waiting," in S.A. Coblentz (ed.), Poems to Change Lives, New York Association Press, 1960.

Cousins, Norman, Anatomy of an Illness, Toronto: Bantam, 1981.

Craig, Mary, Blessings, New York: Morrow, 1979.

Derum, James P., Apostle in a Top Hat: Frederick Ozanam, New York: All Saints Press, 1962.

de Sales, Francis, Introduction to the Devout Life, New York: Doubleday, 1989.

Dickinson, Emily, "Hope," Complete Poems, Part I, London: Faber, 1970.

Drummond, Henry, The Greatest Thing in the World, Toronto: Hodder & Stoughton, 1918.

Fuchs, Emil, Christ in Catastrophe, Wallingford: Pendle Hill Pamphlet, 1949.

Gandhi, Mahatma, All Men Are Brothers, Paris: UNESCO, 1958.

Groote, Gerhard, The Imitation of Christ, New York: America Press, 1937.

Haskins, Minnie Louise, "The Gate of the Year," in The Desert (privately printed), 1920.

Hillesum, Etty, An Interrupted Life, New York: Holt, 1996.

———, Letters from Westerbork, New York: Pantheon, 1986.

Hood, Barbara, and Rachel King (eds.), Not in Our Name: Murder Victims' Families Speak Out Against the Death Penalty, Cambridge: Murder Victims' Families for Reconciliation, 1996.

Hugo, Victor, *Les Misérables*, Harmondsworth: Penguin, 1980.

Jordan, Clarence, *Cottonpatch Version of Paul's Epistles*, New York: Association Press, 1968.

Kazantzakis, Nikos, *St. Francis of Assisi*, New York: Ballantine, 1962.

Keller, Helen, *The Story of My Life*, New York: Dell, 1961.

Kelly, Richard M., *Thomas Kelly: A Biography*, New York: Harper & Row, 1966.

Kelly, Thomas A., *Testament of Devotion*, New York: Harper, 1941.

King, Martin Luther, *Why We Can't Wait*, New York: Signet, 1963.

Kubler-Ross, Elisabeth, *Of Death and Dying*, London: Tavistock, 1973.

Moltmann, Jurgen, *The Power of the Powerless*, San Francisco: Harper & Row, 1983.

Morris, Ruth, "Loving Farthest Out," *Friends Journal* (May 1982).

———, *The Risk of Loving*, Argenta: Argenta Friends School Press, 1978.

Morris, Ruth, and Marie Ottosen, *Journey to Joy*, Red Deer: Cortland, 1986.

O'Neill, Cherry Boone, *Starving for Attention*, New York: Continuum, 1982.

Penn, William, *Some Fruits of Solitude*, Richmond: Friends United Press, 1978.

Pike, Diane Kennedy, *Life is Victorious*, New York: Simon & Schuster, 1976.

Pile, Stephen, *Book of Heroic Failures*, London: Viking, 1989.

Raynolds, Robert, *The Sinner of Saint Ambrose*, Indianapolis: Bobbs-Merrill, 1952.

Seneca, Lucius Annaeus, *Letters from a Stoic*, Harmondsworth: Penguin, 1969.

Siegel, Bernie, *Love, Medicine & Miracles*, New York: Harper, 1998.

Simonton, O. Carl, *Getting Well Again*, Toronto: Bantam, 1984.

Steere, Douglas V., *Doors into Life Through Five Devotional Classics*, New York: Harper, 1948.

Tagore, Rabindranath, *Gitanjali*, London: Macmillan, 1913.

Teresa of Avila, *The Way of Perfection*, London: Sheed & Ward, 1977.

———, *The Interior Castle*, Garden City: Doubleday, 1961.

Thoreau, Henry David, *Walden and Civil Disobedience*, Boston: Houghton Mifflin, 2000.

van Dyke, Henry, *The Story of the Other Wise Man*, New York: Harper, 1923.

Vanier, Jean, *Tears of Silence*, Toronto: Griffin House, 1970.

Weatherhead, Leslie, *Prescription for Anxiety*, London: Hodder & Stoughton, 1966.

———, *The Will of God*, New York: Abingdon, 1964.

Whittier, John Greenleaf, *The Poetical Works of John Greenleaf Whittier*, London: Henry Frowde, 1898.

Wiesel, Elie, *Night*, Toronto: Bantam, 1960.

Wilder, Thornton, *The Eighth Day*, New York: Harper & Row, 1967.

Wilson, Dorothy Clarke, *Take My Hands: The Remarkable Story of Mary Verghese*, New York: McGraw-Hill, 1963.

About the author

RUTH MORRIS was a member of the Society of Friends (Quakers). Ruth spent all her career in community development and working to reform the criminal justice system. In the summer of 2001 she was awarded the Order of Canada — the highest commendation in the country — for her work. Ruth died in September 2001 from a cancerous tumor named Henry.

Ruth Morris (right) and Ruth Bradley-St-Cyr at the 9th International Conference on Penal Abolition in Toronto, May 2000.

About the editor

RUTH BRADLEY-ST-CYR worked with Ruth Morris on several of her book projects, including *Stories of Transformative Justice* and *The Case for Penal Abolition*. When it became clear that she couldn't finish this one, Ruth Morris asked her editor to finish it for her. Ruth Bradley-St-Cyr has been an editor since the age of fifteen and a writer since the age of eight.

AGMV Marquis

MEMBER OF SCABRINI MEDIA

Quebec, Canada
2005